THE FINANCIAL PHYSICIAN

How to Cure Your Money Problems and
Boost Your Financial Health

By Louis Scatigna, CFP
With Mark Steisel

CAREER
PRESS

Franklin Lakes, NJ

THE FINANCIAL PHYSICIAN
EDITED AND TYPESET BY DIANA GHAZZAWI
Cover design by The DesignWorks Group
Printed in the U.S.A. by Courier

To order this title, please call toll-free 1-800-CAREER-1 (NJ and Canada: 201-848-0310) to order using VISA or MasterCard, or for further information on books from Career Press.

CAREER
PRESS

The Career Press, Inc., 3 Tice Road, PO Box 687,
Franklin Lakes, NJ 07417
www.careerpress.com

Library of Congress Cataloging-in-Publication Data

Scatigna, Louis.

The financial physician : how to cure your money problems and boost your financial health / by Louis Scatigna.

p. cm.

Includes index.

ISBN 978-1-60163-098-8

1. Finance, Personal. 2. Finance, Personal--Psychological aspects. I. Title.

HG179.S263 2010
332.024--dc22

2009040488

To my wife, Susan.

Thank you for always believing in me and
for filling my life with abundant love and friendship.

ACKNOWLEDGMENTS

I want to thank Mark Steisel, who worked at an amazing pace to make this book possible. Thanks, Mark, for your patience and guidance. It has been a joy writing with you.

My heartfelt thanks to my family for their love, support, and encouragement: my mother and father, MaryAnn and Leonard Scatigna, who have given me the tools to be successful in life; my brothers Mark, Jim, and Bobby; and my sisters, Terri Kelly and Jennifer Souza. I would also like to thank my mother-in-law, Lynn Grant, for the gift of her daughter.

Thank you to all my associates at AFM Investments, especially my partner, Martin Saltzman, who took the wheel while I was home writing. I would be lost without the following people: my executive assistant these past 15 years, Evelyn Tieto, who keeps me together; the always dependable Judy Lubov; my assistant John Howard Fusco; and Sue Piscioneri. Thanks for all your help and support.

To Suzanne Hilton, who was instrumental in starting me out in radio nine years ago and encouraged me to write this book, thank you for your motivation and abundant enthusiasm. I also thank Bryan Sorensen for his assistance with both the production of this book and *The Financial Physician* radio show. To my friend Peter Grandich, who taught me the value of marketing and was the first to put me in front of a camera and microphone, I learned from the best!

Thanks to my agent, John Willig of Literary Services, Inc., for his confidence in me and in this book. A huge thank-you to everyone at Career Press for giving me the opportunity to instruct others on how to become financially fit.

To Mark Victor Hansen, I appreciate your mentorship, expertise, and remarkable book promotion conferences.

A special thanks to my children, Matthew and Michelle, for being the light of my life. I will love you both until the end of time.

Finally, to my wife, Susan: words are insufficient to express my unending thanks. You possess an amazing patience and love, and are an angel sent to me and our entire family.

CONTENTS

FOREWORD

When Charles Dickens wrote in *A Tale of Two Cities*, "It was the best of times, it was the worst of times," he could have been referring to today's tumultuous economic times. Although we are mired in a steep financial downturn, you can make it *the best of times*—if you know what to do. In *The Financial Physician*, my friend, Lou Scatigna, tells you exactly what to do.

The Financial Physician is a practical, hard-hitting, and indispensable book that should be in every home and office. It's the new financial almanac, the comprehensive reference book we all need to get into top financial shape. The book is packed with tons of critical information that tells you how to turn the tragic to magic. By following Lou's clear, no-nonsense advice, you can cure your money problems, get back on your feet financially, and become and remain financially fit.

Personal finances is a huge area that can be complex and bewildering. It involves many topics: saving, investing, debt, major purchases, insurance, and spousal teamwork, to name just some. *The Financial Physician* covers all the bases; it demystifies personal finances and makes it clear and easy to understand.

Unlike so many other books that concentrate on a few financial issues and leave you scratching your head, *The Financial Physician* covers the 20 most common financial issues people face. On each subject, *The Financial Physician* gives you answers, new understanding, and step-by-step instructions on precisely what you should do.

ABOUT LOU

Lou Scatigna is the right person for these times and this task. He is a highly successful financial advisor who knows the ropes, all the ins and outs of personal finance. A maestro of finance, Lou has been advising and making money for his clients for more than 25 years. He knows how to win in every market—stocks, securities, bonds, mutual funds, annuities, precious metals—and any and every financial instrument, including barter.

Lou also understands safety, security, and people's special needs. He knows what it takes to stay afloat, to save for tomorrow, and to build enough funds for your retirement dreams. Lou is a realist who is willing to go against the grain. Before the 2008 stock market crash, when most "experts" were encouraging everyone to invest, Lou pulled his clients *out* of the stock market and put them *into* safe, money-making investments.

Lou is also a master communicator and teacher. As the acclaimed host of a popular financial radio show, Lou answers questions from listeners on a wide variety of personal finance subjects. He gives answers that tell it like it is and provides solutions that work. Lou's advice is practical, not theoretical. It's based on his years of constant research, extensive experience, know-how, great insight, and unquenchable desire to help others. Lou realizes that life is not just about making money, but he understands how important having money is.

When it comes to personal finance, Lou has done and seen it all. He's a self-made millionaire who knows how to quickly get to the heart of the matter, clearly get his points across, and give advice that people can actually follow and use. In *The Financial Physician*, he clearly explains exactly what you must do and what to avoid in these difficult financial times.

THE BOOK

As a bonus, *The Financial Physician* is beautifully written and a joy to read. It uses only clear, straightforward, non-technical language that everyone can follow. Its analogies to physical health also make *The Financial Physician* a book that you will quickly grasp, remember, and be able to actually apply.

I'm delighted to heartily recommend the *The Financial Physician*, because I know how much it will help you. Read it, refer to it, and follow its advice. Give it to your children; pass it on to your family and friends. *The Financial Physician* will help you solve your financial problems and enable you to reach robust heights of financial well-being and health.

—Mark Victor Hansen, co-creator of the #1 *New York Times* best-selling series Chicken Soup for the Soul, coauthor of *Cracking the Millionaire Code*, *The One Minute Millionaire*, and *Cash in a Flash*, and author of *Richest Kids in America*.

Introduction

For most of my 25 years as a financial advisor, I've been a Certified Financial Planner. In that time, I've met with thousands of clients and witnessed the pain and suffering ignorance inflicts. For 10 years, as the host of a top-rated radio program on finances, I've answered questions for thousands of callers and discussed their concerns. In the process, I've developed a unique approach.

When I first tried to advise people, many didn't understand, or resisted my suggestions. So I decided to try a different technique. I became the Financial Physician and began explaining finance by using analogies to physical health. Suddenly, they understood. I emphasized that physical and financial fitness are both crucial and that their financial well-being is second only to their physical health.

Medical analogies have enabled me to get my message through in ways people could quickly understand and accept. Talking about finances in terms of health lowered their resistance and helped them see the light. They became more open and willing to learn. Their newfound knowledge made them thirst for more; they became eager, cooperative, and active in their role in charting their own financial lives.

HEALTH AND FINANCES

Physical and financial health share many similarities, but substantial differences also exist. Let me explain.

When it comes to physical health, the options are clear. Everyone knows the big picture: exercise; avoid smoking, drinking, and eating poorly; keep stress at a minimum. Although those facts are drummed into us, how many of us do what's best? Fortunately, we usually have a safety valve. When medical problems arise, our bodies let us know. So we hustle off to the doctor, because we know of medical resources and where to turn for help.

With finances, most of us are also aware of the big picture: limit our spending, watch our debt, save, and invest. But with finances, ignorance and resistance intercede. Most people don't have financial safety valves; they don't know what to do or whom to see. If a metaphorical, financial "limb" isn't broken or their "blood" isn't gushing out, they don't seek help. They keep on spending, maxing out their credit and excavating deeper holes. Their pain may be excruciating, but they won't seek help unless they're close to death. And by then, it may be too late.

Good financial well-being can help us enjoy long, productive, and happier lives. Poor financial health can damage our physical health and jeopardize our futures.

THE PROBLEM

Most people know little about finances and have no direction or plans, and don't try to learn about money, fiscal planning, saving, or investing. They live from payment to payment and month to month; whatever it takes to get by. In dealing with finances, they rely on their instincts and on tips from inexperienced friends, and dubious articles or radio and TV pundits. Many blindly follow the advice of stockbrokers and insurance agents, who are salespeople working for brokerage, banking, and insurance firms on a commission basis, and have an inherent conflict between their clients' and their own interests.

In contrast, wealthy individuals are acutely focused on their finances. They know the amount of their net worth down to the penny, as well as how it's invested and how much it should earn. They understand markets and investments, and they are as devoted to making money as athletes are to maintaining their competitive edge. Wealthy people are in the business of making money; they work at it. They read, study, learn, hire top advisors, and stay actively involved.

Ironically, financial fitness isn't hard to achieve. It involves learning some essential concepts that are logical and easy to understand—if properly explained. Financial health also requires planning, discipline, and continued attention. Unfortunately, many of those in the financial establishment—individuals who are in business to make money, not to educate—have made learning about finances too complex. Understandably, most folks are intimidated and remain in the dark.

To enjoy a healthy financial life, people must learn how to manage their money and then actually do it. They must approach it as preventive medicine to build their financial muscles and increase their financial strength. Just as they must exercise and eat right to bolster their bodies and brains and prevent illness, they must learn how to improve their finances and then take control to maintain good financial health.

In *The Financial Physician,* I examine the 20 most common causes of financial problems—mistakes that you, I, and millions of others make. I explain what each ailment is and what causes it, and provide suggestions on how you can avoid it or fix it.

My Hope

When you read my recommendations and put them in place, please be patient, put work into solving your financial ailments, and don't get discouraged. The solutions I recommend have all been tested and truly do work. They will start you on a new path that initially may seem strange, uncomfortable, or even impossible. Don't give up, keep trying, and stick with it, because, if you do, you will truly enhance your life.

If you have questions or comments, please feel free to contact me at lou@thefinancialphysician.com. Send me your personal stories and insights. I'm interested in what you have to say and would love to hear from you.

CHAPTER 1
FINANCIAL ILLITERACY

THE AILMENT

Would you sit down at a high-stakes poker table in Las Vegas if you didn't know how the game was played? Of course not! If you did, you would be throwing your money away. In the beginning, you might be lucky and win a few hands, but, in no time flat, your ignorance would catch up with you, and you would lose your shirt.

Well, every day, millions of people do something just as inconceivable. They go through life without understanding money and finances. They try to make ends meet, pay their bills, fulfill their families' needs, buy homes and cars, and save and invest, even though they have little or no knowledge about what they're doing. So many of them fail—unnecessarily.

Because most of us have never been taught how to manage our personal finances, many of us are financially illiterate.

DIAGNOSIS

During our schooling, we are taught all sorts of subjects, many of which we rarely use. We learn about ancient civilizations and mythology, but not about the basics of managing our money. Although managing our money is an essential skill we constantly must use, it's not a part of most school curriculums. In short, when it comes to money, most of us don't know what to do.

Moreover, the subject of money and finance is made to seem complex, confusing, and beyond our grasp. When we first learn about it, most of us find it intimidating, so we're not drawn to it. Many of us either hope that others will manage money for us, or think that we can always learn about it at a later time, but few of us ever do.

Financial illiteracy is the reason why most people don't accumulate wealth. It's also why they make financial mistakes, fall in debt, can't provide for their loved ones, and jeopardize their futures. Getting into financial trouble is easy; people have lost all their money because they made just one financial blunder. In fact, the National Foundation of Credit Counseling, the nation's largest and longest-serving national nonprofit credit counseling network, counsels more than 3/4 of a million people each year on bankruptcy. It estimates that 25 percent of those it counsels attributed their financial problems to the fact that they didn't know how to manage their money.

VITAL SIGNS

When it comes to their finances, most folks don't know what they're doing; they don't know how to figure out what they can afford, or the best ways to buy, save, and invest. Much of the present financial crisis occurred because people took out mortgages that they didn't understand and subsequently couldn't repay. They couldn't tell when they were being "sold," being put into no-win situations, or given poor advice.

Nearly half of all Americans live from paycheck to paycheck, often because they don't understand how to manage their personal finances. They are only one or two paychecks away from being broke. They have no wiggle room for the emergencies and unexpected expenses that always pop up.

TREATMENT

Become more educated; learn about basic economics. (I bet if you asked 10 people what the GDP [gross domestic product] is, only one or two would know!) To start out, become acquainted with the concepts on the next few pages, all of which I'll discuss in detail in this book.

Investing

I regularly see people who have hundreds of thousands of dollars at risk, but do not understand where that money is and how that investment works. My first job is to educate them and encourage them to learn on their own. Like them, you must learn investment basics. If you don't, you can't take an active role in managing your own investments. You can't make decisions on how to invest your own money and will be forced to rely on others.

At the least, all investors should know the basics about stocks, bonds, mutual funds, and annuities. Specifically, they must understand the advantages, disadvantages, and costs involved for each, such as commissions, penalties, and surrender fees. Finally, they must know how to measure the risks involved.

Credit and debt

When used properly, credit is great, because other people's money can help you get rich. An example of good credit is low-interest, fixed-rate mortgages that are used to acquire property that increases in value. For example, if you can put down 20 percent of the price of a property, borrow 80 percent of the price, and the value of the property increases, that is an excellent use of credit. (Unfortunately, as the value of their properties has gone up, too many people have refinanced them and used the equity to fund consumer purchases.)

The best example of bad debt is credit cards. Credit card debt is a cancer to the financial body. Most credit cards charge high rates of interest, but, despite that fact, many people use them to support themselves or buy items that they cannot afford, really do not need, and should not buy.

Insurance

Although insurance accounts for 10 to 15 percent of most people's expenses, most know little or nothing about it. You don't have to become an expert, but learn the basics of insurance. Most people I see have either too much, too little, or the wrong type of insurance; they don't understand it and how it should be used. Few shop around to find the best values. Consequently, they tend to have the wrong deductibles and pay the wrong premiums for the wrong types of life insurance.

Taxes

Most people are so fearful of the IRS and so ignorant of tax laws that they pay others to do work that they easily could do themselves. Many could have prepared their own tax filings, while others might have noticed costly mistakes that their tax preparers made. Because taxes take a portion of our wealth, we should all manage our money in the most tax-efficient way. To do so, we must understand deductions, tax-free investments, tax-deferred investments, and other strategies that enable us to keep more of our money. The more money we can keep, the more we can invest for our futures.

Estate planning

Many people die without having written a will or having done any estate planning. They have made no provisions or left no instructions on what should be done when they die. Estate planning can ensure that your money will go where you wish, and it can decrease taxes and red tape for your survivors. Unfortunately, most people are not financially prepared to die, and leave their families with time-consuming and costly messes that easily could have been avoided.

Goal-setting

Few people have a structured financial plan; they live their lives on the fly. If they can save some money, they do—but, usually, they can't and they don't. Most people don't say, "I'll save $300 every month and put it into a mutual fund portfolio that will pay for my retirement," nor do they set aside specific sums for each of their children so that they will have the money they need to pay for their college educations. They don't put money aside to pay for vacations; instead, they charge them on high-interest credit cards.

You can't get to your financial destination if you don't know where you want to go. Determine how much money you want for the future. It could be money for the down payment on a home, your children's education, investments, an emergency fund, your lifestyle, or your retirement nest egg. Then, set specific financial goals, write your goals down, and live with discipline to achieve your goals.

Goal-setting helps us lead more financially disciplined lives. If we know that we have firm objectives, we will be more inclined to work to achieve them. Realistically, all your goals won't be fully achieved, but if you achieve some of them, or better yet, most of them, you will be well ahead of the game. You will be saving or investing some, rather than saving or investing nothing and then trying to scramble when it may be more difficult or too late.

Keep current

Stay up to date on finances and the economy. Pay attention to the economic developments that are reported in the media. News and information affects your investments and impacts your financial planning.

Things change, and, when they do, they can provide money-making opportunities for those who see them coming and are prepared to act. Follow the news and developments in finance, tax legislation, unemployment, inflation, housing starts, politics, and market performance. Learn what's going on in your locale and in your areas of interest. Form alliances with people who can be your investment partners.

Become more disciplined

It's old advice that is seldom followed: don't spend money unless you have it. Because most people don't plan financially for the future, they spend without thinking what tomorrow will bring. Unfortunately, the future comes very quickly and catches them off guard. When it does, they may be well past their peak earning years and may be unable to acquire what they need.

Money carelessly spent now on unnecessary purchases can be, with some discipline, set aside for more important expenses later. For example, if you don't start saving for your child's college education until he or she is 14 years old, it may be too late. Even if you can pull it off, it will take a major effort that may leave you with little money for anything else. However, if you start when your child is 1 year old, you can put in less, and let it build and compound.

Gaining financial literacy

Becoming financially literate isn't difficult, but most of us don't put in the effort to educate ourselves in this domain. Moreover, many are afraid that they won't be able to understand what they have to do or think that they lack the discipline to live a more financially healthy life. Instead of this avoidance of finances, help yourself become financially literate by:

- ☑ Reading books and publications on finances. Many excellent books can teach you basic personal financial management.

- ☑ Keeping up with financial news. Read the business section of local and national newspapers. Read the *Wall Street Journal*, *Barrons*, the *Financial Times*, and other publications. Listen to and watch finance programs on radio and television. Some stations on cable television and satellite radio are devoted exclusively to money and finance.

☑ Taking courses. A wide gamut of courses is available in colleges, universities, and community and adult-education programs. Many of these courses are inexpensive and will prove to be a good investment.

☑ Following Internet sites and blogs.

☑ Finding financial advisors whom you trust and asking them to explain anything you don't understand.

☑ Spending time with people who are interested in finances and have dealt with them successfully. Talk with them about your finances, ask questions, and pick their brains.

☑ Joining financial and investment clubs.

My Rx

For most people, the financial crisis has been a wake-up call. It has forced them to begin learning more about and paying attention to their financial situations and their futures. In the new financial landscape, people will need to become more frugal, more goal conscious, and more financially literate in order achieve their goals.

Financial literacy is an ongoing process. Once you gain some initial knowledge, you'll want to keep up. It will become an interest, a fascination that you enjoy and incorporate as a regular part of your life and which will help improve its quality.

CHAPTER 2
BEING FINANCIALLY IRRESPONSIBLE

THE AILMENT

When we hear the term *financial irresponsibility*, we tend to think it means not paying our bills, buying extravagant items that we can't afford and really don't need, and taking on far too much debt. Yes, those are examples of financial irresponsibility, but it also is much more. Let me give you an example:

> Alex and his wife, Betty, each smoke two packs of cigarettes a day. At $7 per pack, they spend $28 on cigarettes each day. Alex also drinks two six-packs of beer a day, which adds another $14 a day. So between cigarettes and beer, they spend $42 each day, $294 a week, and $15,330 a year. If you compound this through the years, you're looking at a great deal of money.

This example may seem extreme, but, believe me, it's not. Many Alexes and Betties, people with expensive vices, exist. Their vices wreck their financial health and damage their physical health, which will cost them even more in the long run. The money they spend on their vices could be used to pay off their debts, to build their wealth, and to enable them lead more comfortable lives. Instead, it's being wasted, going up in smoke.

DIAGNOSIS

Financially irresponsible people spend more than they earn. They buy homes, cars, furnishings, and clothing that are more than they need and can afford. As they make more money, most expand their lifestyles, but don't increase their savings or their wealth. When they get raises, they travel more, buy bigger homes and nicer cars, and spend more freely. They do not understand the basics of financial management. Despite making more money, they fall further into debt and destroy their finances.

On the other hand, responsible individuals learn about economics and money management. They find out what's involved and keep up to date with what is happening in the world. They learn to whom they can turn for help and continually watch and manage their money. They spend and save carefully.

Read, study, and educate yourself. The more education you acquire, the more you will learn about finances and how to boost your financial health.

According to CNN Money & Main Street, education has a strong correlation to unemployment. Of people over age 25 who are unemployed:

☑   15.47 percent have no high school diploma.

☑   10 percent are high school graduates.

☑   7.72 percent have some college or an associate's degree.

☑   4.76 percent hold a bachelor's degree or higher.

Many young people drop out of school. Others complete high school, but don't go further. When they decide to discontinue their education and go out in the world, many of them don't understand the full implications involved—even though they think they do.

Not getting a higher education immediately puts most young people behind the eight ball, and they can't really compete. From the moment they stop going to school, finding jobs in which they can advance, earning enough to live comfortably, and working in careers that they love all become more difficult to achieve.

On the other hand, college graduates get better jobs, earn better incomes, and tend to do more interesting and meaningful work. Their educations set the stage for the rest of their lives. Most people who do not attend college *never* catch up.

VITAL SIGNS

Personal responsibility and financial responsibility go hand in hand; they're inseparable. People who are not personally responsible are almost always financially irresponsible. Financial responsibility equates to maturity—growing up and behaving like a mature, responsible adult.

Most Americans, regardless of their age, tend to act financially immature. Instead, we must exert self-control and self-discipline. We must live within our means. Better yet, we must live *below* our means in order to accumulate enough money to have comfortable futures.

We Americans have the wealthiest lifestyles in the world, but we save at rates that are among the lowest in the world. In Asia, savings average well over 10 percent per family, whereas savings in the United States has been mired in the low single digits.

Many families, instead of controlling their finances, allow their finances to control them. Rather than working with what they have, they try to imitate what their friends and neighbors do and how they see people on TV, in the media, and the movies spend their money. They overextend themselves by trying to live extravagant, fairy-tale lives they can't afford and which put them in situations that soon become beyond their control.

Treatment

To become more financially responsible, follow these steps:

☑ Learn the basics of financial management.

☑ Seek out people who enhance your education. Identify top experts who can advise and guide you.

☑ Take a systematic approach to your finances. Make a financial plan, a budget, so you know what you can spend. Set parameters for your spending and stick with them. Keep good records and routinely check your budget to make sure you're on track.

☑ Cut out all money for needless expense such as vices when you write your budget. Giving up smoking, drinking, gambling, drugs, and other vices can be exceptionally hard, but it's the first big hurdle you must clear to regain your financial and physical health. It's the acid test that you have to pass if you want to build wealth, enjoy good health, and have a comfortable future.

☑ Apply the "need test" before you buy anything. Ask yourself if you need the item or service, not merely want it. If you don't truly need it, don't buy it. Get into the habit of cutting back. Eliminate all your excesses and buy only what you truly need.

☑ Change your partners in crime, those playmates who encourage your irresponsibility and wanton ways. They're bad influences, aiders and abettors, and not true friends. If they were true friends, they wouldn't encourage you to take the road to self-destruction.

☑ Grow up. Realize that it's time to turn the corner and become an adult. Acknowledge that being an irresponsible kid was a blast while it lasted, but now that time has passed. Now, it's time to change. Take responsibility for yourself and for your behavior, and become the best, most responsible person that you can be.

My Rx

It is impossible to be financially healthy when you're financially irresponsible—you must be either one or the other. If you really want to build your net worth and have no money pressures, commit to living responsibly—financially and personally. I know that it can be difficult to change, but becoming financially and personally responsible is the only way you can become financially fit.

Personal responsibility goes hand in hand with financial responsibility. When you take control of your physical body, it usually transfers to your financial health as well. The vast majority of people who smoke, drink, gamble, or use drugs have continual financial troubles. Control *all* aspects of your life, take charge, become more responsible, and watch your financial situation improve. Clean up your entire act!

CHAPTER 3
FEELINGS OF MATERIAL ENTITLEMENT

THE AILMENT

When I was growing up, my parents, five siblings, and I lived in a small house. Although our quarters were close, we made it work. Our family had one car, which we kept until it died. Every night, we all sat down for dinner together. On the rare occasions we ate out, it was to celebrate a special event. When I was a kid, we took only one vacation: we all got in the car and drove to Niagara Falls.

Money was always tight, so our family lived frugally and watched what we spent. My parents only bought what we needed. We didn't have credit cards, so we had to live within our means. When we wanted to buy something for ourselves, we frequently had to save for it, which took a while, or we bought it "on time."

Today, people live totally differently; they have a different attitude. They're driven by feelings of material entitlement. They believe that they deserve to live extravagant lifestyles—the type of lives they see in movies, magazines, advertisements, and on television—which most of them can't afford. To get what they think they deserve, they spend all they have, erode their savings, and plunge into debt.

People today are also impatient and unwilling to wait. Because they won't hold off until they can afford what they want, they put it on plastic, on their credit cards. By feasting today, they risk starving tomorrow.

At no time in history have any people lived as we Americans have been living for the past 30 years. We act as if we are extraordinarily wealthy people with unlimited funds and buying power. Now that we are in an economic downturn, millions are paying a steep price for living the high life and with such abandon.

DIAGNOSIS

Buying material goods and living extravagantly is expensive. Ironically, by buying excess amounts of consumer items, people aren't building their net worth. Instead, they are creating unhealthy patterns in which they're constantly pressed for funds.

Easy credit has been a major culprit. It helped create a culture in which millions of people are encouraged to live beyond their means. The credit industry preys on their feelings of material entitlement and insistence on immediately getting what it took their parents years to acquire.

For instance, I've seen a number of recent college graduates driving luxury cars that took their parents decades to afford. Car by car, their parents worked their way up the auto chain, progressively buying nicer and more expensive vehicles. However, right off the bat, these young people buy or lease brand-new, luxury models. As I point out in Chapter 14, "Wasting Money on a Lifetime of Cars," buying expensive new cars is a costly financial mistake.

Because they have feelings of entitlement, people use credit to purchase what they can't afford. And the use of credit is the main reason why people fail financially.

VITAL SIGNS

Typical symptoms of feelings of material entitlement include:

☑ Buying homes that are bigger and more luxurious than needed. In most cases, the larger the home, the more it costs to buy, furnish, maintain, heat, cool, light, and insure. Plus, the property taxes of larger homes are higher.

☑ Frequently buying new, luxury cars. Similar to large homes, luxury cars cost more to buy or lease, finance, run, repair, and insure—and they tend to be less energy efficient. Getting a new car every few years wastes money, because today's cars are built to run much longer. The large gas-guzzlers that were so popular a few years ago cost a bundle to run and are now murder to unload.

☑ Dining out several times a week and frequently buying take-out food. Eating at home is much cheaper and much healthier—physically and financially. Bringing your lunch to work instead of eating out can save you hundreds of dollars a year.

☑ Taking frequent vacations. At least once a year, many families take vacations, whether they can afford it or not. Frequently, they travel long distances to exotic resorts and locales. In addition, they often take shorter trips throughout the year. Traveling is expensive, and the cost of frequent vacations mounts up—especially because most are charged to credit cards.

☑ Shopping and buying unneeded items. For many people, shopping is entertainment or retail therapy. It also can be wasteful, because many purchases are made on impulse, not because of need. Shoppers often accumulate closets and attics full of stuff that they barely use.

TREATMENT

Live a simpler, more disciplined life that is within your means. Differentiate between what you need and what you want or feel you deserve. Try this exercise; it can help change your attitude:

1. Itemize how you spend your money. List every expense you pay each month (for example, $100 each month for cable television).

2. After you list each of your expenses, evaluate each and circle those that you could cut back on or eliminate, such as those premium cable channels that you rarely watch.

3. Calculate how much you could save on each circled item.

4. Add up how much you could save in total. The average family can often lower their expenses by 5 to 10 percent.

Eliminate waste in your life. If that means downsizing your home, cars, and lifestyle, think seriously about doing so. Realize that, in the future, you may no longer have the earning power that you have today. Determine what you want your lifestyle to be in the future and how much that would cost. Then start planing how you can fund the future you want.

MY RX

So how did we get into this fix? I think that advertising, movies, and television changed our culture. By constantly inundating us with alluring images of how we should live, they implanted unrealistic standards in our minds. They painted such a rosy picture, made it look so easy and so attainable, that we were completely drawn in.

Because these images were with us constantly, they became ingrained in our culture. We bought it all and abandoned the common sense lessons we were taught. We lost sight of the fact that we were being sold by brilliant salespeople whose messages saturated our lives. Even if some of us resisted, they got to us through our children, friends, and neighbors. They made us crave their goods and surrounded us with pressure.

It takes strength and courage to swim against the tide and fight massive forces that want to consume us—especially when what they tell us is so appealing. But hang in there! Know that you're not alone and that the bind you might be in is not all of your own doing. It's not too late to change your attitude, become more responsible, and regain your financial health.

Chapter 4
Addiction to Debt and Spending

The Ailment

In the late 1970s, traditional commercial banking practices began to change. Before then, loans were primarily given on a local basis: local banks lent money to local individuals and commercial customers. By the late 1970s, large lending institutions moved in, and lending became a huge, nationwide business. These institutions began to grant personal loans throughout the country. The vehicle they used most was credit cards.

Lending institutions relaxed their standards in order to extend more personal credit. They stopped investigating loan applicants as carefully and lent money to people they previously might have rejected. Lenders aggressively solicited credit card customers. Many of them had no or poor credit ratings. Before long, virtually everyone had credit cards—a lot of them.

Obtaining personal mortgages also became easier. A new cycle was introduced: lenders started bundling their mortgage loans and selling them. Bundling occurs when investment banks take hundreds of mortgage loans and make a security (bond) out of them. Those securities are then sold as mortgage backed securities. As a result, the lenders that granted the mortgages are no longer subject to any loss or liability if any of the individual mortgages go into default. When borrowers defaulted, the lenders were no longer on the hook, which decreased their incentive to closely scrutinize the credit worthiness of new mortgage applicants. The cycle was completed when the lenders took the funds they received from their bundled mortgage sales and issued new mortgages, which they then bundled and sold.

As credit became easier to obtain and more widely available, the public began buying more. Much of what they purchased was items they didn't need, but wanted. Soon, we became a nation of spenders.

Simultaneously, another change was taking hold. As people earned more money, they didn't put it in the bank. They increased their spending and their lifestyles. Instead of saving or investing, they took their extra money and bought larger homes, bigger cars, and more expensive furniture. They also traveled more, ate out more, and lived more lavishly.

Not only had Americans become addicted to spending, but they charged much of what they spent. A generation grew up believing that spending and assuming more debt was normal, acceptable, and what they should do.

DIAGNOSIS

With the availability of easy credit, shopping has become a pastime, an activity to occupy and entertain us. We love the process of buying and acquiring things. It's fun, it keeps us busy, and, for many, it became an addiction. The most obvious symptoms of our addiction to spending and debt are buying what we don't need, impulse purchasing, and toting around wallets bulging with plastic.

Charging unnecessary purchases has become a way of life. It's quick, easy, and, at the point of purchase, its relatively painless because it doesn't immediately drain our bank accounts. That comes later.

According to myFICO (*www.myfico.com*), the average consumer has a total of 13 credit obligations on record at a credit bureau. These include credit cards (such as department store charge cards, gas cards, and bank cards) and installment loans (such as auto loans, mortgage loans, and student loans). Of these 13 credit obligations, nine are likely to be credit cards and four are likely to be installment loans.

Vital Signs

Credit cards are a cancer that destroys the financial body, and the malignancy is spreading. More than 700 million credit cards were reportedly in circulation in the United States in 2008, and the debt on those cards came to $2.5 trillion. Whew!

In the depth of the financial crisis, many credit card companies have jacked up their rates. The interest on some cards has reached exorbitant levels. Credit card issuers have also made many of their terms stricter. Some have reduced credit lines, whereas other have been increasing their interest rates when payments are even one day late. Still others have been boosting their rates for customers who were late paying *other* bills.

As we spend and charge, we fall deeper in debt. Even if our earnings increase, our net worth doesn't grow, because we buy on credit and pile up more debt. Because we have to pay hefty amounts of interest, we have little or nothing left to save and invest.

In fact, according to the Federal Reserve Board, family debt levels in the United States are nearly double what they were 25 years ago. Debt has risen at a far faster rate than the economy has grown, so our economy is now debt-driven. For example, in 1985, total household debt was $400 billion; in 2008, it soared to $13.8 trillion. This includes $10.5 trillion in mortgages and $2.6 trillion in credit card debt.

Another staggering statistic is that in 2006 and 2007, for the first time, Americans had a negative savings rate. That means we spent more than we earned. The following chart illustrates how our rate of saving has tumbled.

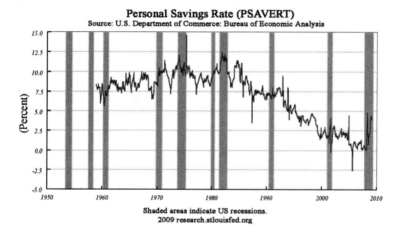

Personal Savings Rate (PSAVERT)
Source: U.S. Department of Commerce: Bureau of Economic Analysis

Shaded areas indicate US recessions.
2009 research.stlouisfed.org

TREATMENT

Cure your addiction to debt and spending by buying only what you absolutely need, not what you just want. Go cold turkey, be more disciplined, and stop all impulse buying—even when you're food shopping. Don't tempt yourself by visiting shops or malls to hang out, kill time, or amuse yourself. In fact, don't go to shops and malls unless you:

- ☑ know beforehand exactly what you need.
- ☑ really need that item.
- ☑ leave as soon as you buy what you sought. Don't purchase anything else, dawdle, or look around, because the temptations may be too much for you.

Pay credit card debt

Paying off credit card debt is easier when you have a structured plan. Take the following steps to get rid of your debt:

1. Review what you owe on all your cards and identify those cards that charge the highest interest rates.

2. Focus on the card that charges the highest interest rate. Lets call it "Card A." Pay as much as you can more than the minimum to reduce your balance on Card A.

3. For all your other credit cards, just pay the minimum payment until you fully pay off Card A.

4. When Card A is paid off, begin to pay as much as possible above the minimum on Card B, the card that now has the highest interest rate. As you reduce what you owe on Card B, keep making minimum payments on all your other credit cards.

5. When you pay off Card B, continue the process with Card C and work your way down until you pay off all of your credit card debt.

Let's look at the steps again, this time with some specific examples.

The following table shows the balances to be paid, the interest rates, and the minimum payments for each card. Notice that the card with the highest interest is listed first.

	Balance	Interest Rate	Minimum Payment
Card A	$3,000	23%	$75
Card B	$3,500	18%	$88
Card C	$1,500	15%	$38
Card D	$2,500	10%	$63

If your total budget for credit card payments is $600 per month, then pay $411 each month on Card A and minimum amounts on all others, as shown in the following table:

	Payment	Months Until Paid Off
Card A	$411	8
Card B	$88	
Card C	$38	
Card D	$63	

When Card A is paid off, pay $499 each month on Card B and minimum amounts on all others:

	Payment	Months Until Paid Off
Card B	$499	7
Card C	$38	
Card D	$63	

When Card B is paid off, pay $537 each month on Card C and the minimum amount on Card D.

	Payment	Months Until Paid Off
Card C	$537	3
Card D	$63	

Finally, when Card C is paid off, pay $600 each month until Card D is paid off.

	Payment	Months Until Paid Off
Card D	$600	3

Some experts advise debtors to first pay off their credit card with the smallest balance so they get the satisfaction of eliminating that debt in the shortest amount of time. These experts advocate this approach because they think it will allow debtors to pay off one credit card quickly and motivate them to continue paying their other credit card debt.

Paying off cards with the smallest balance first may be a strong psychological motivator, but getting rid of the highest interest rate first is the soundest, most cost-efficient financial decision.

Either way, choose an approach and stick with it. Both approaches work, but, again, only if you stick with them. Because eliminating your credit card debt will take time, it's critical that you take a systematic approach to reduce your debt each and every month until it disappears.

Make large payments whenever you can. Use tax refunds and any other windfalls you receive to pay off your highest-interest credit card. Get out of debt as soon as possible, so you can begin building wealth by saving and investing.

Don't miss any payments. Find some way to pay something, even if it's just a token payment. If you can't make as large a payment as you planned, don't throw in the towel. Pay what you can and try to make up for it in subsequent payments.

When all your credit card debt is paid, make a firm commitment to pay for everything in cash and not to charge anything. Cut up all your credit cards except one or two that you may need to use in emergencies or for the rare occasions when cash isn't acceptable. And make sure to close those accounts. Better yet, only use debit cards, so your charges are immediately deducted from your account, and you don't incur any interest charges.

If, after you have paid off all your cards, you have to charge purchases to a credit card for any reason, pay the amount you charged in full during the payment period, which is usually 30 days. If you make timely payments, you won't incur any interest costs, and you will build a strong credit rating.

Keep track of your credit rating

A good credit rating is critical. It's the financial equivalent of a strong pulse. Having strong credit is essential to your financial health, because you never know when you might want or need to borrow money.

Your credit rating may also influence those who are considering selling or renting to you, doing business with you, or hiring you. If you have a good credit rating, you frequently can get lower interest rate loans.

Credit ratings are compiled by three credit-reporting agencies:

☑ Equifax (*www.equifax.com*) (800) 685-1111.

☑ Experian (*www.experian.com*) (888) EXPERIAN or (888) 397-3742.

☑ TransUnion (*www.transunion.com*) (800) 680-7289.

Once a year, you can get a credit report from each of the credit-reporting agencies at no charge. Each report contains the information that particular agency has in your credit file, such as your payment history and existing debt. For a nominal fee, Equifax and TransUnion will also give you your FICO score, which I will describe. Once a year, sites such as *www.annualcreditreport.com* will give you your credit reports from all three at no cost.

Every four months, I check my credit with a different agency. That way, I am only requesting a report from each agency once a year. When I check my credit, I make sure that the debt listed on the report is mine and that no errors have been made. If an error appears, I can quickly try to get it corrected before any damage is done.

FICO scores

The most widely used credit score is the FICO score, which are compiled by the Fair Isaac Corporation. Fair Isaac compiles three

FICO scores, one for each of the credit agencies. For each of the three, Fair Isaac uses only the information in your credit report with that agency. Although Fair Isaac uses the same information for each agency, your FICO score may differ from agency to agency because each may have different information on you. That's why it's important to check your credit scores with each agency.

FICO scores range from 300 to 850:

- ☑ More than 750 = Excellent
- ☑ 720 to 750 = Very Good
- ☑ 660 to 720 = Acceptable
- ☑ 620 to 660 = Uncertain
- ☑ Below 620 = Risky

The best way to build your credit score is to:

- ☑ Pay your bills on time.
- ☑ Keep low account balances.
- ☑ Consistently pay more than the minimum to decrease your balances.
- ☑ Keep your oldest credit cards active, use them occasionally, and promptly pay their balances.
- ☑ Check every bill and dispute all errors.
- ☑ Check your credit reports and challenge anything questionable.
- ☑ Before you apply for a loan, don't incur any new credit charges for a month or two.
- ☑ Take new credit only when you absolutely need it.

Paying more than the minimum won't immediately reduce your credit score, because agencies only look to see that you're paying the minimum required. However, in time, it will reduce your balances and that will help to raise your score.

The Credit Card Accountability, Responsibility, and Disclosure Act

As I write this book, a new law was enacted to force credit card companies to end some of their most egregious practices. Highlights of this new law, which goes into effect in February 2010, include:

☑ Credit card companies must give 45-days notice that they are increasing fees, rates, and finance charges.

☑ If "teaser rates" (low initial interest rates) are offered, they must remain in effect for at least six months.

☑ If credit card companies increase borrowers' interest rates, the increases will apply only to new purchases, not to existing balances less than 60 days past due.

☑ Credit card companies must send borrowers bills no later than 21 days before their due dates.

☑ Payments will be applied first to the balance with the highest interest rate. Prior to the new law, principle payments were applied first to the lowest rate balance.

☑ Credit card companies are prohibited from giving cards to people under 21 years old, unless they apply for a card and prove they, a parent, or guardian can pay their debt. Their credit limit is also capped at 30 percent of that income. (I love this provision. Young adults are often lured into debt, become addicted at a young age, and remain so for the rest of their lives.)

☑ Universal default, which raises the interest on your credit cards if you are late on payments such as utility bills and car payments, is prohibited.

☑ Fees for paying bills by phone or online are eliminated.

Identity theft

With so many credit cards in circulation, and with the easy access that modern technology gives thieves to private information, identity theft is now an epidemic. These criminals go to great lengths to steal your personal information and have developed insidious ways to rip you off. Prevention is your best bet, because once your identity is stolen, it can be a major ordeal to fix.

Of the identity theft reported, credit card fraud accounted for 28 percent, phone or utilities fraud accounted for 19 percent, and bank fraud made up 18 percent. A 2004 Federal Trade Commission study found that thieves most often steal personal information through:

- ☑ Mail theft. Stealing incoming and outgoing mail to get account and financial information.

- ☑ Dumpster diving. Going through the trash at your home and place of business for items containing personal information.

- ☑ Skimming. Storing your credit and debit card numbers in special storage devices that copy those numbers when those cards are processed for sales.

- ☑ Phishing. Pretending to be legitimate financial companies and sending e-mail or pop-up messages to get you to reveal your personal information.

- ☑ Change of address. Completing a change of address form to divert your statements to another location.

- ☑ Stealing. Taking wallets, purses, personal records, and mail. Bribing employees who have access to personal information.

- ☑ Shoulder surfing. Watching from nearby as people punch in telephone calling card or credit-card numbers. Listening to conversations for credit-card numbers that are given to hotels, rental car agencies, or other companies.

☑ Pretexting. Using false pretenses to obtain personal information from financial institutions, telephone companies, and other sources.

Be vigilant. Protect personal information including your Social
Security number, driver's license number, account numbers, credit
card numbers, expiration dates, PINs, passwords, and mother's
maiden name. The following suggestions will help keep your identity, and credit, safe:

☑ Secure your mail, both incoming and outgoing. Use a
locking mailbox or a postal mailbox, especially if you
live in a high-traffic area or if frequently no one is at
your home.

☑ Shred all mail that contains your account numbers or
offers preapproved credit.

☑ Don't give your Social Security number unless it's
absolutely necessary.

☑ Don't carry your Social Security card or number on
your person.

☑ Shred any papers that list your Social Security number.

☑ Make a list of all your credit card numbers and keep
it in a safe place.

☑ Keep your credit cards, debit cards, checks, account
information, and PINs in a safe place.

☑ Use up-to-date anti-virus and anti-spyware software
on your computer.

☑ Never provide sensitive information in response to
e-mail requests.

☑ Never give sensitive information over the telephone
to someone you don't know.

☑ Never click on links or open e-mail attachments if
you don't know where they lead.

☑ Don't save your passwords on your computer.

☑ Frequently check your credit card and bank balances. Because you can review these accounts electronically, do so at least once each week.

☑ Subscribe to an online monitoring service that will alert you to changes in your credit scores.

☑ Check your credit scores with all three credit-reporting agencies. Make sure your scores did not suddenly drop, that no unknown new accounts were opened, and that no large balances or delinquencies were incurred.

☑ Make sure your paper statements arrive on time, and review them.

☑ If a collection agency calls about an unpaid bill, don't assume it's a mistake. Check into it.

☑ Whenever you're asked for personal information that may seem inappropriate, ask how the information will be used, if it will be shared, and how it will be protected. If you're not 100 percent certain, don't reveal any of your personal information.

☑ Don't give personal information that is requested for surveys, interviews, or articles.

My Rx

The rules for using and paying off credit cards effectively are simple, but you need to be committed and disciplined. Work at them, and, before you know it, they will become second nature to you. Eliminating debt is a worthwhile pursuit you should take up immediately, and, once accomplished, is an achievement that will make you proud.

Remember, if used properly, debt is good. If misused, it's a cancer that can wreck your financial health. So buy only what you need, don't charge your credit card needlessly, and keep your debt to a minimum. Avoid all impulse buying. Maintain a great credit score and check it regularly. One lapse usually isn't fatal, so don't use it as an excuse to get off track. Rather, if you lapse, correct the situation right away.

Chapter 5
Failure to Understand Your Financial Psychology

The Ailment

Nothing—not love, politics, sex, or religion—makes people crazier than money does. The most levelheaded people can suddenly become totally irrational when money is involved. For example, when it comes time to pay the dinner check, the wealthiest, most extravagant people may calculate their share down to the last penny.

Our financial psychology determines how we deal with money. It's important to understand our financial psychology, because it will give us greater insights into why we handle our money as we do. People tend to make more financial mistakes as a result of their feelings about money than they do because of the financial realities involved.

Diagnosis

Essentially, we all fall into one of two basic financial psychologies. We may have mild or extreme cases, but we all tend to fit in one of the following categories:

☑ Attitude of abundance. Believing that we have or will always get whatever we need to live a good life and to support our families and ourselves. Those who have an attitude of abundance feel that the world is filled with opportunities and possibilities. I have clients who have little money and don't seem concerned. They never complain about finances, live comfortable lives, take frequent vacations, and are generous. They seem to feel that everything will be fine and that somehow they'll get whatever they need.

☑ Attitude of lack. Believing that you may not have or be able to get whatever you need. I also have clients who are millionaires and have an attitude of lack. They're always concerned that they won't have enough. Many of them are tightwads, compulsive savers who are always worried that they may lose what they have. Most of these people grew up in difficult financial conditions that left a lasting impression they can't shake.

The way we relate to money has more to do with our attitude about life in general than how much money we have. Our feelings of abundance or lack do not correlate to how much we actually have, but are *financial states of mind*. So what are the symptoms of each financial psychology?

Those in the abundance camp tend to invest rather than save. They are not always looking for guaranteed or safe investments and are more prone to taking risks. They feel that if they lose money, they can always make it back. People with an attitude of abundance usually live better lifestyles and fuller lives. They are not averse to spending their money to buy the good things that life has to offer, and don't waste much time worrying about the stock market, their mortgages, and money in general.

Conversely, people with an attitude of lack are always worried that they won't have enough. Deep down, they're afraid that they might have to struggle, so they sock money away to make it through those difficult times. People with an attitude of lack tend to be savers rather than investors. They would be devastated if they lost any money, because they feel that they only have a finite amount. They like to stockpile their money and avoid risk, so they put their money in the lowest-yielding, but safest, vehicles.

VITAL SIGNS

The groundwork for our attitude toward money is laid in childhood. We are as strongly influenced by our parents' attitudes as we are by our family's financial status. Depression Era children, whose parents struggled to put food on the table, naturally have different attitudes toward money than children who grew up in affluent times and environments. Many of us have also been influenced by how we saw our friends, family, and neighbors deal with money. We wanted what they had and wanted to live as they lived, so we adopted their attitudes and tried to copy their behavior. They became our role models.

Our psychology affects how we spend, save, and invest. Some of us are high rollers, gamblers who are willing to always shoot for the moon in the hopes of making a big score. At the other end of the spectrum are the squirrels, frightened investors who are so afraid to lose money that they spend very little and buy only the most conservative investments that bear the smallest returns.

See where you fit in among the most common profiles:

☑ The High Roller
- ✓ Thinks that everything in life is a gamble and wants big returns in a short period of time.
- ✓ Uses high-risk investment strategies and is always looking to hit the jackpot.
- ✓ Incurs big losses because his or her investments lack good diversification and asset allocation.
- ✓ Is bored with conservative, long-term investments and tends to speculate in individual stocks, commodities, and real estate.

☑ The Abdicator

- ✓ Has little or no interest in managing money.
- ✓ Prefers to have someone else handle his or her money and will usually do what his or her financial advisors suggest.
- ✓ Is trusting and often surprised when he or she loses money.
- ✓ Is frequently taken advantage of by unscrupulous characters.

☑ The Credit Junkie

- ✓ Addicted to acquiring things, rather than to building wealth.
- ✓ Is usually in denial regarding his or her addictive spending.
- ✓ Tends to carry big credit card balances.
- ✓ Has little savings or net worth because much of his or her income goes toward debt payments.
- ✓ Wonders why it's so hard to get ahead without realizing the self-sabotage through needless, compulsive spending.

☑ The Squirrel

- ✓ Is as conservative as they come.
- ✓ Does not overspend and lives frugally.
- ✓ Operates with an attitude of lack, because of the fear that he or she will never have enough money.
- ✓ Keeps most of his or her money in banks and treasury bills.
- ✓ Is willing to only get low returns, because he or she finds the stock market too risky and is deathly afraid of losses.
- ✓ Has trouble keeping pace with inflation.

☑ The Money Master

✓ Is obsessed with money management.

✓ Is well educated in all money-related matters, tends to avoid others' advice, and takes full control of his or her investments.

✓ Employs risk controls, but isn't fearful of investing money in a diversified investment portfolio.

✓ Reaches his or her financial goals but also enjoys his or her money success by living an abundant and balanced life.

Treatment

The way we relate to money is a learned behavior that is hard to change. Strangely, when it comes to money, people tend to go to extremes. Many spend their working years saving for retirement, but when they retire, they won't spend any of it—not even the interest generated by their savings and investments. Others spend freely and quickly have nothing left.

I call myself a financial therapist because so much of my job involves helping my clients work out their financial behaviors. Often, I have to convince my retired clients to start spending some of their money. Like squirrels gathering acorns for winter, they've been so conditioned to saving and building nest eggs that they find it difficult to change. The only difference is that squirrels *eat* the acorns during the winter.

On the flip side, I also try to counsel my clients with attitudes of abundance to stop overspending because it will wreck their financial health. Their cavalier attitudes may be fine when they're earning lots of money, but not when that income stream stops or slows. Overspending can be financially fatal.

Wealth is not just how much money we have, it's also how we live. Identify your priorities and decide what's most important to you by answering the following questions: What is true wealth to you? Is it the quality of the food you eat? Being comfortable in your home? Enjoying time with your family and friends? Continually learning and growing? Giving to charity? Does it make sense to accumulate a million dollars, but die without spending any of it?

The dilemma is that you can't take it with you when you die, but you also need enough to live. Solve that dilemma by striking a healthy balance between saving for the future and enjoying life by spending some today. Because each of us differs, decide what *you* want to do.

My Rx

Make a list of things that you would like to do and then plan to do them. Figure out how much they will cost, the time they will take to achieve, and what you will need to accomplish them. This will help you strike a balance between planning financially for the future and spending some money on important projects now.

You can change your attitude about money, but it takes time. Financial therapy, like physical or psychological therapy, usually doesn't work overnight. It takes more than one session, and you have to work on it. Be patient. Don't expect to make a total change and don't expect it to happen immediately. Give it time, expect the results to occur gradually. When they do, enjoy them, because you've earned them.

CHAPTER 6
LACK OF SPOUSAL TEAMWORK

THE AILMENT

Most couples don't talk about money unless the roof is falling in. They live from day to day without making concrete financial plans. When they do discuss their financial goals, their plans tend to be general and don't include specific steps on how they will be carried out. Partners also don't work together to help keep each other on track, and, worse yet, they don't really know what the other wants.

If only one member runs the financial show, the other may feel left out and that he or she has no say in the use of his or her own money. The managing partner may not know what the other really wants nor get the benefit of the partner's knowledge and feelings—which could be considerable. If only one partner has total control, teamwork and unity suffer and divisiveness and resentment can arise. Negative feelings can undermine a couple's relationship. Those feelings can fester, trickle down, and infect the rest of the family and their close friends.

DIAGNOSIS

Domestic relationships have changed. Today, usually both partners work and their combined earnings support the family. Because the family money belongs to them both, each should have a say in handling the family finances. Traditional gender-based roles have also changed significantly, but this is not always the case in managing the family finances. I've found that in most families, one spouse or partner still runs the financial show, and it's primarily the male partner, but that is also changing.

If the partner who handles all the family finances also works, it can be a heavy load for them to bear on their own. As a result, that partner may not devote all the time, focus, and energy necessary to do the best job. The managing partner can make poor decisions, choices that the other partner disagrees with or that may not be in the other partner or the relationship's best interest.

One person doing all the financial work also has an effect on the non-managing partner and on the relationship. The non-managing partner may not be aware of limits that he or she should follow. If unaware that they are in a financial crunch, the non-managing partner may spend freely and drive them further in debt. Likewise, the non-decision-making partner may not understand the reasons for the managing partner's actions, which can affect their relationship by causing misunderstanding and resentment

If the sole financial steward suddenly dies, the survivor may be totally unprepared to step in. I've dealt with survivors who had no knowledge or experience with finances. Some had never written a check. A number were forced to rely on advisors, family, friends, or associates of the deceased, whom they didn't like or didn't have their best interests at heart. Still others fell victim to devious financial salespeople and advisors—sharks and vultures who prey on hapless survivors.

Lets face it: one of the spouses will eventually die. In all probability, both spouses will not die together, and male partners will usually go first. If the survivor has not been involved in the family's finances, he or she can make major financial mistakes, incur unnecessary expenses, or be ripped off.

Planning and working as team is a must. If partners manage the finances together, they can share the load, pick each other up, and do a better job.

VITAL SIGNS

In relationships, we often take on roles, and certain ways of thinking become ingrained. Traditionally, men were the head of their households. They were in charge of their family's money and made the financial decisions. Because men were the primary earners, they usually paid the bills and handled the savings, investments, and future planning. They gave their wives and children allowances and provided household funds.

In some households, a woman's involvement in fiscal matters was considered improper, so they received no financial training and were not included in financial discussions. Many husbands were so secretive that their wives were left completely in the dark. Recently, women have become more involved in their family's finances. In fact, many have taken charge.

Neither partner should have to shoulder all the responsibility or do all the work. Both partners can plan, set priorities and goals, solve problems, and evaluate the risks together. Often, partners balance each other out. For example, one may be financially aggressive whereas the other is financially cautious and conservative. Together, they can find a happy medium.

When potential new clients make an appointment to see me, I ask if they're married. If they are, I make sure that their partner joins them when we meet. Because I will be working with the couple and building *their* wealth, I think it's essential that *both* understand the basics of the family finances, so we can do what is best for them. I also want both partners' input, involvement, and direction.

TREATMENT

It's vital that both partners be on same page about their money issues. They must discuss their finances, set goals, and plan and work together to reach them. When both are involved, they share the burden, as well as motivate each other. They increase their chances of making the most of their money, building wealth, and achieving their financial goals. Working together also strengthens their relationship.

Find out what each of you wants

Partners should talk and find out what each wants. My first objective with new clients is to find out what they want. I ask about how much wealth they would like to build, how long they want work toward this goal, and how they would like to live while they're amassing that wealth. Right up front, I ask them directly. I need to be clear on their objectives so I know what steps to take. However, when I ask, I'm still amazed by how often I hear, "Gee, I don't know. I haven't thought about it."

In any kind of relationship, it's vital to understand the other person's wishes. When you ask your partner what he or she wants, what you find out is often a real surprise. People whom you think you know well may have wishes that are vastly different from what you expected. Never assume that your partner shares your goals or that you know what he or she wants. After all your time together and as close as you may be, you're still different people and may have different wants and needs.

Talk. Don't leave it to chance. Clarify what your partner wants most. Ask your partner directly what he or she would like. Then tell your partner what you wish. Most people never discuss their financial objectives with their partners nor ask what they want most from life. When they finally talk, they frequently find that they have different goals and objectives.

When you know what each of you want, you have a place to start. Identify your shared objectives and build on them. If you're far apart, work to reconcile your differences through compromise. Then plan. Together, figure out the steps you must take, how much each part of your plan will cost, and map out the best route to plan and pay for it.

One conversation is not enough. People change and so do their needs and objectives. In a few years, what you passionately desire today may mean little or nothing to you. As you go through life, events invariably intervene and move us in different directions. Today's dreams may be replaced tomorrow by something you can't even imagine now.

Talk frequently with your partner and discuss both of your wishes. Note how he or she has changed. As things change, review your goals and priorities together. Then make the necessary adjustments so that you can work together to reach each of your goals.

Pay bills together

Two heads are better than one. If both partners are engaged in paying the bills, both will be motivated to trim expenses, stretch dollars, and save and invest in order to build wealth.

When you pay your bills together, also review your savings and investments. Discuss how each is doing, and strategize. Ask if they are producing as expected and if you should change them. Talk about the type of investments you think you should have and the people to whom you should go for advice. Decide who will be responsible for checking out possible investment opportunities or contacting a new financial advisor.

Use the following steps to pay your bills and review your finances:

1. Sit together. Choose a time and place free from distractions.

2. Discuss all the family's bills and pay them. If they're too high, explore how to reduce them.

3. Discuss ways to increase your savings.

4. Review your investments. Talk about how they're doing and the changes you could make.

Accountability

Goals are easier to reach when others support our efforts. That's the beauty of teamwork. If we act alone, it's easy for us to stray and accept our own excuses if we mess up. However, it's much harder to pull the wool over other people's eyes—especially those of partners who are close to us.

If spouses and partners work as teams, they are less likely to drift off course. Partners provide checks and balances and hold each other accountable. They each make sure that the other does his or her share and stays on track.

Partners working together are also more motivated to do well because, instead of just working for him or herself, they are each working for the partnership. If one occasionally falls short, the other can jump in and pick up the slack. They can also motivate, encourage, and help each other to overcome adversity or to resist temptations.

My Rx

When we leave this earth, do we want to leave our spouses in a position in which they are bound to fail financially or to be devoured by sharks? Of course not! We want them to be happy and do well. It is imperative that, at the least, they know the basics of finances so that, when they're alone, they won't make major mistakes and can lead comfortable and financially healthy lives.

The only way to ensure that both of you are financially aware and stable is to work together. Have open conversations about your finances frequently. Be willing to listen and take suggestions. Work together to pay all your bills, review all statements, and build your wealth. Speak with your accountant and financial and other advisors together. Become a team that is dedicated to working together to build your wealth.

CHAPTER 7
LACK OF DETAILED RECORDKEEPING AND REVIEW

THE AILMENT

When you go to your doctor for your annual check-up, your height, weight, and vital signs are checked. You're asked how you feel and if you have any pressing problems, and that information is entered in your chart. Then the doctor reviews your record, notes changes from the previous year, gives you some more tests, and discusses your physical condition with you. Every year, the same process is repeated.

Because we know that our physical health is vitally important, we undergo comprehensive medical examinations each year. We also give our doctor enough information to provide a good picture of our overall condition. However, when it comes to our financial health, few of us are nearly as diligent. Most of us don't keep good financial records, make budgets, or monitor our financial health.

DIAGNOSIS

Not keeping good financial records, checking your accounts, knowing your net worth, or budgeting is financial malpractice. It can easily get you into deep financial trouble. By not keeping track of your finances, you can miss obvious danger signs, irregularities, or dormant symptoms that recently sprang to life. Prolonged negligence of your financial well-being can be expensive to fix.

Think of financial recordkeeping and review as preventative medicine, necessary steps that you should take to stay financially fit. Being financially vigilant can be thought of as a wise investment, because it's far easier and invariably less expensive to spot problems and attack them in their infancy than when they have taken hold or spread.

As the recent financial decline deepened and the stock market nose-dived, millions of people didn't open their financial statements. Deliberately, they buried their heads in the sand, because they were afraid to face how much they lost. They decided that ignorance was bliss, which it seldom is. As a result, they didn't learn the extent of their losses and many didn't spot places where they could have acted to reverse or reduce the pain.

VITAL SIGNS

Most people shy away from financial recordkeeping. They don't like to balance their checkbooks, and the idea of comparing their checkbook registers against their bank statements horrifies them. Some are just undisciplined; others don't care. Many are afraid that they will make mistakes. For years, they have told themselves that they were never good at math or recordkeeping, so they grew up hating and avoiding it.

Ironically, financial recordkeeping isn't difficult, but it takes a bit of time, organization, and attention. If you regularly monitor your finances, you feel proud of yourself and become more interested and engaged. You also become more disciplined. You always feel better when you're aware and in control of where your money is going.

As you become more involved in keeping track of your finances, it becomes easier, and something you might even enjoy, because, when you see improvement, it motivates you and makes you more engaged. When you place money in an account each month, you look forward to seeing statements that show how much your balance has grown. It motivates you to continue investing and building wealth.

If you regularly monitor your accounts, you are more in control of your finances. You can make quick adjustments, such as cutting your losses or seizing on potentially profitable opportunities that often have narrow windows during which you can act.

Programs such as Quicken (*http://quicken.intuit.com*), Quick Books (*www.quickbooks.com*), Moneydance (*http://moneydance.com*), and Microsoft Money (*www.microsoft.com/money*) have made it easier to track finances, and online bill payers can have their payments categorized in areas that can easily be tracked.

TREATMENT

Play a leading role in managing your money. Instead of being a bystander and accepting whatever comes down, get actively involved in charting your financial future.

Start by finding a place to keep all your records and receipts, a spot that's convenient and easy for you to access. It can be a file, folder, drawer, or an old shoebox. Then get into the habit of putting your receipts there each day. Placing everything in one location will help you be more organized and disciplined. When you need any of your receipts or records, you'll know exactly where to go.

Monthly reviews

Each month, review all your financial records, such as bills, financial statements, and 401(k) plans. It probably will take less than an hour. Couples should conduct reviews together as I suggested in Chapter 6.

Keep an eye on changes in your credit. Credit card companies change their interest rates, as well as other terms, including the amount of credit they extended. If your credit line is reduced, your credit rating goes down, because it's based on credit utilization. That means if you have a $10,000 credit line and $2,000 in debt, you've only used 20 percent of your available credit, which will give you a high credit score. However, if your credit card company lowers your available credit to $4,000, your $2,000 debt will then be 50 percent of your line, so you will receive a much lower score. A lower score will make it harder for you to get credit and can increase the amount of interest you will be charged on future loans.

Monitor your investments to check know how well each of your investments is performing. Make sure that your strategy is working and that you're properly diversified. Compare how your investments are doing in comparison with the market in general. If the market is down 30 percent this year, your investments probably won't be doing well. If your loss is less or equal to the market in general, your investments will most likely be sound. But if your losses are greater than those of the market in general, something may be amiss. Try to find out why your investments are underperforming, and adjust.

When you review your investments, ask yourself:

☑ How did I do with this investment last month?

☑ What was the rate of return?

☑ Could I have made more if my money was invested elsewhere? If so, how much?

Few people monitor and make adjustments in their 401(k) plans. Many don't remember how they invested that money and don't keep track of how it's performing. As a result, they don't make the necessary adjustments when they should.

Monthly financial review checklist

When you conduct your monthly review:

☑ Examine every bill and statement line by line.

☑ Compare the amount of each charge with your receipt to make sure it is accurate. (Bills can be wrong; charges can be in error. Interest rates may have been raised, so you might want to stop using certain cards. If you have questions on any item, immediately contact the company that billed you.)

☑ Question whether each of your expenditures was necessary.

☑ Ask if any expenditure (such as a phone service) is too expensive and whether you could buy it for less at another company.

☑ Check your interest rates, lines of credit amounts, and the balances available to you.

☑ Note when each bill must be paid.

☑ Monitor all your investment accounts for performance, diversification, and risk.

☑ Check your bank statements for your savings levels and interest rates.

☑ Compare your actual expenditures to your written budget.

☑ Consider tax implications of any transactions you completed in the past month (such as capital gains, taxable distributions from retirement accounts, and large employment bonuses).

Net worth statements

Each year, prepare a net worth statement that tells you how much you own and how much you owe. Your net worth statement is your scorecard, your financial report card. It breaks down all your assets and liabilities, and tells you the total amount of money you're worth. If you were to sell everything you own and pay off all your debt, your net worth statement would tell you exactly how much money you have.

Your net worth statement is the most important document you should complete each year. If you want to build wealth, you want your net worth to increase each year. That means that you're saving more money, paying down debt, your investments are growing, or all three.

Use this Net Worth Worksheet as a basic template for preparing your net worth statement.

NET WORTH STATEMENT

Name: _____

As Of: _____

ASSETS		LIABILITIES	
Checking	$ _____	Mortgage	$ _____
Savings	_____	Credit Cards	
CD 1	_____	Card 1	_____
CD 2	_____	Card 2	_____
		Auto Loans	
		Car 1	_____
		Car 2	_____
Total		**Total**	
Assets	$ _____	**Liabilities**	$ _____

Investments

401(k) $ _____

Investment
Account 1   _____

Investment
Account 2   _____

IRA 1   _____

IRA 2   _____

Other   _____

**Total
Investments** $ _____

Fixed Assets

Home $ _____

Other Property   _____

Car 1   _____

Car 2   _____

Total Fixed
Assets $ _____

**TOTAL
ASSETS** $ _____

**NET WORTH
(Total Assets
Minus Total
Liabilities)** $ _____

Income and expense statements

Each year, we also need to prepare an income and expense statement—a budget. To many, "budget" is a dirty word. To others it's their battle plan to prosperity, because it tells them exactly what they can spend. An income and expense statement lists the amounts of money we received from all sources and how and where we spent it.

In your income and budget statement, keep track of everything you spend, including how much you pay for your mortgage or rent, car payments, utilities, food, vacation, clothing, and eating out. Take note of any spending that was wasteful, including money spent on vices such as smoking, drinking, gambling, and drugs, as I discussed in Chapter 2.

When preparing your budget, make sure to allocate funds to save and/or invest. Determine how much you can save or invest by subtracting your expenses from your income. The amount left over is what you can save and/or invest.

If you don't have money left over for savings, see if you can increase your income. Also, review each of your expenses and see what you can reduce or eliminate in order to build your net worth. See where you can apply more money to saving, investing, or paying down your debt. To find where you can cut your expenses, review your back bills, your current checking accounts, and all of your statements, including ATM withdrawals. Then try to adjust your budget, so you have money to save and invest each month.

Be completely honest in preparing and adhering to your budget. If you're not totally honest, you will only be fooling yourself. Couples should prepare the family budget together.

Although budgets seem restrictive, they actually are very helpful because they give you a game plan, blueprints that you can follow and review to see if you're on course. By telling you what you can spend, budgets show you how you can achieve your financial goals.

Fine-tune your budget as your conditions change (for instance, when you make more money or decide to save for a home, your kids' educations, or a piano). Review your budget. See where your money could be better spent and then adjust your budget accordingly.

Regularly check to see if you're staying on budget, and, if you've strayed, decide how you can get back on course. In the beginning, check whether you're staying on budget every couple of weeks. After a while, do it once every month or two. Soon, you will know if you're on track without having to look at your budget.

Use this Cash Flow Worksheet to help prepare your budget:

CASH FLOW STATEMENT

Name: _____

As Of: _____

INCOME	MONTHLY	ANNUALLY
Salary (Net After Taxes)		
Partner A	$ _____	$ _____
Partner B	_____	_____
Interest	_____	_____
Dividends	_____	_____
TOTAL INCOME	$ _____	_____

EXPENSES	MONTHLY	ANNUALLY
Fixed		
Home Mortgage (Include tax and insurance) or Rent	$ _____	$ _____
Car 1 Loan	_____	_____
Car 2 Loan	_____	_____
Partner A Life Insurance	_____	_____
Partner B Life Insurance	_____	_____
401(k)	_____	_____
Education fund	_____	_____
Variable		
Utilities	$ _____	$_____
Clothing	_____	_____
Groceries	_____	_____
Gasoline	_____	_____
Travel/Vacation	_____	_____
Entertainment	_____	_____
Eating Out	_____	_____
Misc.	_____	_____

**TOTAL
EXPENSES** $ _____ $ _____

**Positive/Negative
Cash Flow
(Total Income
Minus Total
Expenses)** $ _____ $ _____

My Rx

Conduct your monthly financial review when you pay your bills. At that time, you're focused on your expenses and how much they're costing you. You're also more engaged in your finances, so it will be natural to also check your investments and other finances to get an overall picture of your financial situation.

When you prepare your net worth statement, also prepare your budget. It will be easier to create a budget once you've seen how your wealth has grown and have all of the information needed at hand.

When you create your budget, don't be overly restrictive. Leave enough money to enjoy life. Keep enough for entertainment, to travel, and go out to eat, but don't splurge. Be responsible and find the right balance between living an enjoyable life now and saving enough for an enjoyable life in the future. Understand that you may have to make some sacrifices, but have faith that they will be well worth it.

CHAPTER 8
RELYING ON UNQUALIFIED FINANCIAL ADVISORS

THE AILMENT

We're bombarded by tips and financial advice that can cost us lots of money. We get them from friends, family, television personalities, media pundits, and financial gurus. We're told to invest in hot trends or bubbles involving certain companies or industries. Unfortunately, much of this advice is bad or comes too late.

Then there's inside information: The brother-in-law of a woman who works at X Corporation gives your Uncle Jack a tip about a revolutionary new product that X Corporation is about to launch. According to the brother-in-law, "It will sell like hot cakes and just can't miss." So you, Uncle Jack, and half your family buy X Corporation's stock, the new product bombs, and you lose big.

Advice from professionals such as stockbrokers and financial advisors can also be dicey, especially if they work on a commission basis. Many financial advisors receive a commission on every transaction they make for their clients: when they buy and sell, regardless of whether those investments make or lose money. So the advisors can't lose, even though their clients often do.

DIAGNOSIS

Blindly acting on advice from others can be a sure way to lose money. Before you invest, investigate financial advisors and investments. Find out who you can trust to advise you on how stock markets work and about specific industries in which you may invest.

To familiarize yourself with the financial world, read publications such as the *Wall Street Journal*, *Barron's*, the *Financial Times*, *Money*, *Business Week*, and *Forbes*. At first, you may feel as if you're reading a foreign language. Stick with it and it will quickly begin to make sense. You'll learn a great deal.

Check the Internet; lots of great information is available online. Market Watch (*www.marketwatch.com*), which is owned by Dow Jones, provides comprehensive financial news, commentary, and market data. Other good sources are Yahoo Finance (*www.finance .Yahoo.com*), MSN Money (*http://moneycentral.msn.com*), CNN Money (*www.money.cnn.com*), and Bloomberg (*www.bloomberg.com*).

Listen to my weekly radio program, *The Financial Physician*, on XM Satellite Radio, WOMB-AM, and on the Internet at *www. thefinancialphysician.com*. Listen to *Moneytalk with Bob Brinker* (*www. bobbrinker.com*). Watch Bloomberg Television for 24-hour financial news and *Nightly Business Report* on PBS.

VITAL SIGNS

People are impressed by titles, which is why nearly 100 different financial-advisor designations now exist. The requirements for these titles differ greatly. Some take years of initial education, experience, and continuing education, whereas others only mean that someone has taken a three-hour course. In other words, don't be misled by an advisor's title.

Unfortunately, it doesn't take much to get a license to sell mutual funds or other securities and call yourself a financial advisor. Additionally, the fact that a person or firm is licensed or registered does not guarantee success. Get recommendations and investigate any advisor before you do business with him or her.

It's crucial to know what different financial-advisor titles mean and the qualifications for each. It can help you to decide whom to work with. Because so many financial advisor titles exist, I've highlighted few of the major designations, as well as some weaker ones. For information on other designations see *www.wiseradvisor.com/designations.asp* or *http://apps.finra.org/DataDirectory/1/prodesignations.aspx*.

Major designations

Certified Financial Planner (CFP)

This is the most prestigious financial-advisor designation. The basic requirements for a Certified Financial Planner include:

- ☑ Having 3 years experience in the financial services industry and a bachelor's degree, or 5 years of financial planning experience.
- ☑ Passing a two-day exam that covers financial planning, taxes, insurance, estate planning, and retirement.
- ☑ Maintaining high ethical conduct.
- ☑ Completing 30 hours of continuing education every two years.

A CFP will understand all of the major financial categories: investments, insurance, estate planning, corporate benefits, retirement, and income-tax planning. He or she should be able to advise clients on most of their financial dealings and concerns. A CFP will know and can recommend other experts, such as lawyers, accountants, and insurance professionals.

Because most CFPs are also registered representatives, working with a CFP may not cost more than dealing with a general stockbroker.

Registered representative

Registered representatives are also known as stockbrokers or account executives, and will often refer to themselves as "financial advisors." However, they are essentially securities salespeople who are not required to have had financial-planning training. Most work for brokerage firms licensed by the U.S. Securities and Exchange Commission (SEC) and various stock exchanges. Registered representatives earn commissions on the securities they buy and sell for clients, so make sure that their recommendations are based on your financial interests, not theirs. To become a registered representative, candidates must:

- ☑ Be associated with a stock-exchange member broker/ dealer firm.

- ☑ Pass securities exams. Exams differ based on the type of securities in which they wish to deal. Passing Series 7 Exam allows salespeople to sell general securities such as stocks, bonds, mutual funds, and variable annuities. Those who pass Series 6 Exam can sell only mutual funds and variable annuities.

- ☑ Be registered with a member of the Financial Industry Regulatory Authority (FINRA) or a self-regulatory organization (SRO).

- ☑ Be licensed in each state in which they conduct business.

Selling variable annuities requires at least a Series 6 securities license and a license to sell life insurance. Life insurance licenses are issued and regulated by the states, not the federal government.

Registered Investment Advisor (RIA)

A Registered Investment Advisor is an individual or a firm that receives compensation for providing advice on securities and must register with the SEC and/or state securities agencies as an investment advisor. Most RIAs charge management fees based on a percentage charged on the amount of assets they manage. In some instances, RIAs will also be registered representatives, selling investments, and charging a commission.

Current law states that advisors managing $25 million or more in assets have to be registered with the SEC, whereas those who manage less must register with their state's securities department. Investment advisors who are associated with a broker/dealer are usually exempt from registration, because they are mainly sales agents and fall under FINRA regulation.

Insurance agents

Insurance agents must be licensed by the states in which they sell life, health, property and/or casualty insurance, and fixed and variable annuities. Exclusive agents only sell insurance products for one company, whereas independent agents sell insurance products issued by more than one company. (Insurance coverage, which is also referred to as risk management, should be a part of your comprehensive financial planning.) Insurance agents also sell annuities, an investment-like, tax-deferred account that also has life insurance features.

Chartered Life Underwriter (CLU)

A Chartered Life Underwriter is the most respected and prestigious designation in the insurance industry. Candidates must take five courses in life insurance and financial planning that concentrate heavily on life insurance laws, regulations, and ethics. In addition to their life insurance expertise, CLUs tend to be well educated in estate planning techniques. To maintain the CLU designation, 30 hours of continuing education is required each year.

Weak designations

The following designations can be obtained with little effort and should be considered more as marketing tools than as evidence of ability, education, or experience. A number of states have taken actions to regulate the use of designations that they deem deceptive.

Certified Senior Advisor (CSA)

Offered by the Society of Certified Senior Advisors, this designation implies that the advisor is well educated in senior financial matters when, in fact, the curriculum only takes 3 1/2 days (or self-study) followed by an exam. It's hard to believe that all that is needed to learn about the complexities of senior financial issues can be accomplished in only a few days.

Certified Senior Consultant (CSC)

Offered by the Institute of Business and Finance, this designation also implies a high degree of training in senior financial management. The designation is earned after completing only 25 to 30 hours of self-study and passing three final exams. Continuing education requirements are 15 hours per year for the first five years.

Certified Fund Specialist (CFS)

To be certified for this designation, an applicant only has to take a self-study course and pass three short exams. An applicant can receive this designation even though he or she is not licensed to sell mutual funds, and does not have any continuing education requirements to maintain this designation.

How advisors are paid

Financial advisors are paid in two primary ways: by (1) fees based on the value of the assets being managed or the time spent on the account, or (2) commissions on transactions they handle for their clients. In some cases, advisors may receive both fees and commissions.

Traditionally, the finance industry has been commission-based, but recently that's been changing. Because how your advisor is paid can affect his or her performance, here are some pros and cons about each payment method that you should consider.

Fee only

Fee-based financial professionals charge an hourly fee for the time they spend on their clients' accounts, or annual fees based on the amount of assets they manage for clients. Their compensation increases according to the growth of assets they manage, so they have more incentive to try to put their clients in investments that will do well. Advisors that earn more if their clients make money and less when their investments lose value.

If advisors are fee based, they can be more objective and honest in their decisions, because their compensation is not based on how much or how often they buy and sell for their clients. They can focus on the quality of their recommendations, as opposed to how often they can get their clients to buy and sell. Usually, fee-based advisors do not have to meet sales quotas, and they may be more immune to pressure from their firms, because their firms do not have interests in the sale of specific products.

Fee-based advisors are less likely to be caught in conflicts of interest that can arise when they recommend products that pay high commission rates but may not be suitable for their clients. Because fee-only advisors don't receive commissions, they tend to use low-cost, no-load mutual funds and annuities—products that have low management fees and give their clients access to their monies without costly penalties.

Commission-based

Most investment brokers (registered representatives) and insurance agents work on commission. Commission-based advisors must continually sell financial products to earn a living. As a result, commissioned advisors have been known to scour their clients' accounts in times of need in order to find investments that they can turn over to generate income for themselves and/or to meet their firms' quotas.

Most commissioned advisors are honest and ethical, but they are constantly subjected to strong temptations that may seduce them into selling products principally because they have high commission rates. A good example occurred during the past decade, when the sales of variable annuities soared because they paid high commissions—not because they were such great investments for most of their purchasers.

When you're making your decision regarding whether to hire a fee- or commission-based advisor, factor in these two facts: Most of the complaints that are filed against financial advisors are against those who are commission-based. Also, commission-only advisors turn over ("churn") their clients' investments more frequently, which can require their clients to pay lots of commissions.

Fee and commission advisors

These advisors are the double-dippers; they charge hourly or annual fees while also earning commissions on the investment products they buy and sell. Fortunately, most advisors either charge fees or take commissions and don't double dip.

TREATMENT

Take responsibility for the management of your money. Educate yourself about money and investments so you can make, or at least actively participate in making, the best, most informed decisions for yourself. You don't have to become a financial expert; you just have to get a basic understanding of what is involved.

Interviewing prospective financial advisors

Hire the best, most competent financial advisors. Get names and recommendations from your friends, relatives, and business associates. Sit down and meet personally with all the candidates. Question them. Don't be bashful, and remember that you will be entrusting your advisor to make important financial decisions.

See if you feel that you can speak comfortably with them, if you trust them and feel confident about them. Determine whether they understand your situation and will make the best recommendations for you

Use the following checklist as a guide for your interview. Then add specific questions that may be important to you. When you question candidates, make sure that you fully understand their answers.

- ☑ What specific service will you provide me with?
- ☑ What are your specific objectives for my account? Please prioritize them.
- ☑ How do plan to reach those objectives, and in what time frames?
- ☑ How else should I measure results?
- ☑ How are you compensated?
  - ✓ By commission on products sold?
  - ✓ Hourly fees?
  - ✓ Fees based on a percentage of the value of the assets you will manage for me?
- ☑ Do you anticipate any special problems with my account? If so, please state what they are and how you plan to handle them.
- ☑ Who other than you will work on my account?

- ✓ What is his or her experience?
- ✓ To what extent will he or she work on my account?
- ✓ Will you supervise him or her? If so, how?
- ☑ Do you have good working relationships with outside experts, such as accountants, lawyers, and insurance specialists, who can help with my finances?
- ☑ How much access will I have to you?
- ☑ How much access will I have to others who work on my account?
- ☑ What is your preferred communication method: phone, e-mail, or in person? Please explain.
- ☑ Will you contact me for approval before making any decisions on my account?
- ☑ How often can I expect to hear from you about my account?
- ☑ How often will I get printed or online account statements?
- ☑ What can I do if I don't receive the results promised?
  - ✓ Can I fire you?
  - ✓ Will you refund fee payments? If so, how much?
  - ✓ Will will you work to resolve the problem at no charge?
- ☑ What specific results have you created for past, similar clients?
- ☑ Who can I contact as references for you? Please provide at least five names and their contact information.
- ☑ What are your strong points and your advantages over other financial advisors?

My Rx

A good financial advisor is as essential to your financial health as a good physician is to your physical health, so choose wisely. Hire a knowledgeable, well rounded, and respected financial advisor, one who has a good knowledge of estate planning, taxation, insurance, law, and other related fields in addition to his or her investing expertise. Be sure that you:

- ☑ Feel comfortable with the advisor you select.
- ☑ Have easy access to the advisor, and he or she returns your calls promptly.
- ☑ Communicate well with your advisor.
- ☑ Trust that person to advise you on your finances.

Top financial advisors help their clients with everything in their financial lives, including how they should buy their homes, the types of mortgage they should obtain, and the right type of financing for their cars. Finding a well qualified advisor who can assist in these matters will greatly aid your financial health.

Even if you have a good advisor, don't invest in anything without conducting your own independent research. Find out as much as you can about the asset you may buy. Don't blindly follow tips or advice, even from those with whom you have a long and successful relationship. Remember: their money is not on the line, but yours is! If an investment goes south, you, not your advisor, will feel the pain.

CHAPTER 9
SAVING INSTEAD
OF INVESTING

THE AILMENT

Saving may seem like an obvious way to build wealth, but if money is put in low-yielding savings accounts, rather than in investments, it's not being used to its full potential. People who put most of their money into their savings tend to be cautious. Frequently, they feel that they worked hard to accumulate their wealth, and they don't want to lose any of it. For many, their greatest fear is running out of money, so they place their funds in the safest, most conservative investments and don't increase their wealth.

Being financially conservative makes good financial sense to a point; that point is where it ends up costing you money. When you save and get low returns, it costs you dearly. Being overly cautious doesn't make good financial sense. Rather, it gives you a false sense of security.

DIAGNOSIS

The purpose of savings is to accumulate funds for emergencies and to have liquidity, easy access to your money. Savings should also be used to build and hold money for purchases that you plan on making within six months or a year. For example, if you're going to buy a home, you wouldn't invest your down payment, so you put it in a savings account where you can quickly access it. In contrast, the purpose of investing is to make money and build wealth.

Savings accounts are safe. Your money is insured, so you're not going to lose any of it. However, compared to most investments, your rate of return will be extremely low. Investing, on the other hand, involves risks. Luckily, because so many types of investments are available, the risks can be kept to a minimum, and your funds can grow.

Unfortunately, too many people are so financially conservative that they place everything in savings accounts and consider them their investments. For example, they buy Certificates of Deposit (CDs), which are safe but have meager yields. If a CD made 4-percent interest, its yield would be less than *the real rate of return on your money.* (The real rate of return is the amount your money earns, minus taxes and inflation.) Say you buy a CD that pays 4-percent interest annually. If you pay 25 percent in taxes, your after-tax return on that CD would be 3 percent. If inflation is 5 percent, your real rate of return is -2 percent. That means that your purchasing power has decreased by 2 percent annually, and, when compounded in time, it becomes a recipe for disaster. That's why I call CDs "certificates of depreciation," because they frequently don't keep up with the annual inflation rate.

VITAL SIGNS

If you make safe, conservative investments, your wealth will grow in time. The trick is to have your money continually working for you so your earnings compound.

If your money compounds, it can make a big difference in the long term, as illustrated by the following chart:

COMPOUND GROWTH CHART

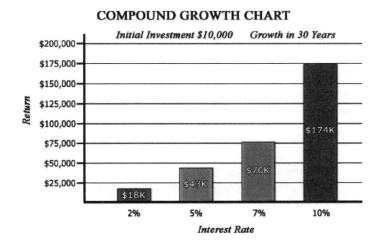

Time is crucial, because the sooner you invest, as opposed to just saving, or, worse yet, spending, the more your investment can grow. Start as early as you can, even if you invest only small amounts.

Though investing is crucially important, it's also how people make their biggest financial mistakes, because they lack sufficient knowledge, or, as I discussed in Chapter 8, they rely on the wrong advisors. In the pages that follow, I'm going to give you a brief introduction to the most common types of investments.

Stocks

When you buy corporate stock, you own a portion of publicly traded corporations—usually a miniscule portion because corporations issue millions of shares. When you buy corporate stock, you're betting that the company will do well, that its sales will rise. As it does, more people will want to own shares, the company may pay higher dividends, and the price of its shares will increase and may even split. Buying corporate stock is attractive because your gains receive special tax treatment—your profits are taxed at a lower rate than the ordinary income rate.

The type of corporate stock most frequently traded is common stock. Most common stocks are traded on public exchanges, so they are liquid, which means that you can easily sell them and get your money. Common stocks usually provide voting rights and pay dividends.

Preferred stocks also convey ownership in a corporation, but they operate more like bonds. They guarantee to pay a certain rate of interest. Some preferred stock can be converted to common stock. If the company goes bankrupt, preferred shareholders are paid before common stock owners. Preferred stocks don't increase in value as much as common stocks (which is why they include a convertibility feature), so they don't have as much capital gain up-side potential as common stocks. However, they do pay higher dividends and provide a bit more safety.

Mutual funds

Mutual funds are large diversified pools of money, typically hundreds of millions of dollars that are invested into hundreds of securities. Instead of investing all of your money in one stock, you can buy mutual funds, which are far more diversified and have less risk. Mutual funds are professionally managed and monitored by people who are supposed to be investment experts.

Thousands of mutual funds are available. They may have different objectives and specialize in a wide variety of areas. One mutual fund may buy only blue chip stocks, whereas another may deal exclusively in shares of small companies. Some funds buy only overseas stocks; others purchase only shares of technology companies. Some will buy only U.S. government bonds, municipal bonds, or corporate bonds.

I prefer to buy mutual funds rather than stocks in individual companies, because funds have less risk and I can buy a wide range of different types of mutual funds. They allow me to take a strong position in an industry or sector of the economy that I think is going to take off. If I invest $20,000 in five mutual funds, I will own 1,000 to 2,000 different securities. I don't have to worry about my money disappearing the way it could if I bought shares only in single companies, such as Bear Stearns, Lehman Brothers, or Enron.

Mutual funds expose you to less market risk. If the entire market goes down, so will your mutual funds. However, you don't have the same level of risks as you would if you invested in just one company's shares.

Different types of mutual funds exist. With open-ended funds, you buy shares, and the fund is always issuing shares. Closed-end funds generally don't continuously offer shares for sale. Instead, they initially sell a fixed number of shares at the initial public offering and then trade on a stock exchange.

Exchange traded funds

Exchange traded funds (ETFs) have become increasingly popular. ETFs are index funds, baskets of different securities that trade on the stock exchange like a single stock. In contrast to mutual funds, which you can only sell at the end of the day, you can buy and sell ETFs at any time during the day.

ETFs are highly focused. An ETF may only deal in shares of companies in medical technology or gold mining companies—companies that issue certain types of corporate bonds. ETFs have low management costs, often less than 0.25 percent per year, and are very liquid. Because most ETF portfolios are pretty static, they don't involve many capital gains transactions and can have tax advantages. A drawback of ETFs is that you must buy and sell them through brokers, so you have to pay a commission for each ETF sale or purchase.

Bonds

Bonds are loans that pay a stated amount of interest. Bonds are issued by a number of sources including corporations, the federal government, state governments, local government units, and public utilities. You can also buy bonds issued by foreign entities.

Corporate bonds

If a company needs money for such things as expansion or building new facilities, it will issue bonds and raise capital from investors. The bonds it issues will have a stated rate of interest and will mature at a certain term in the future. Investment-grade corporate bonds are conservative investments. Bond prices fluctuate from time to time, but not nearly as much as publicly traded common stocks. If a corporation that issued bonds goes bankrupt, bondholders are paid first, before preferred and common shareowners.

Government bonds

Government bonds or U.S. Treasury bonds are certificates of debt guaranteed by the U.S. government. They pay fixed rates of interest and mature in as little as one month (T Bills) or in as long as 30 years (Treasury bonds). The longer the term, the higher the yield you should receive. The market price for U.S. Treasury bonds fluctuates based on interest rates. If interest rates rise, the price of U.S. Treasury bonds declines.

For example, if, after you buy a newly issued, 20-year U.S. Treasury bond for $10,000 that yields 4 percent, and the market rates rise to 7 percent, you may want to sell your 4-percent bond and buy a new 7-percent bond. However, no one will pay you $10,000 for your 4-percent bond when they can get a 7-percent bond. Therefore, if you wanted to sell your bond, you would have to take considerably less money. The market value of your bond will be determined by the amount of time left before it matures.

The opposite is true if interest rates decline. The market value of existing U.S. Treasury bonds will rise in value. Bonds operate like the seesaws in a playground. As interest rates go up, bond prices go down, and vice versa. As you move to the center of the seesaw, the fluctuation decreases, because the bond will soon mature and you can reinvest the money you receive at the prevailing rate.

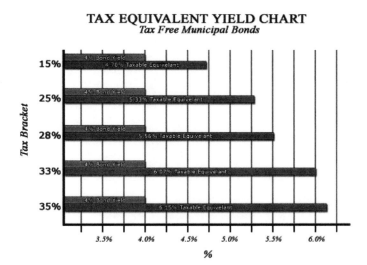

TAX EQUIVALENT YIELD CHART
Tax Free Municipal Bonds

The risk in investing in government bonds is related purely to rising interest rates. When you buy a bond, your hope is that the interest rate won't climb.

Municipal bonds

States, cities, and municipalities issue municipal bonds. When the U.S. government was formed, the states agreed not to tax the U.S. government's bonds, and the federal government reciprocated by agreeing not to tax state and local bonds. Consequently, when you buy municipal bonds, you pay no federal taxes on the earnings and no state taxes if you live in the state where those bonds were issued.

The movement in interest rates affects the value of municipal bonds. Another potential risk is that the state or municipality's finances deteriorate and it defaults on its bonds. However, that risk is rare.

Annuities

An annuity is a tax-deferred investment account offered by insurance companies. When purchasers invest in annuities, the money that they pay is distributed in periodic payments, which can start immediately or at specified times in the future.

I'm not a big fan of annuities. I call them the roach motels of investment: you can get in, but you can't easily get out. Annuities charge high management fees, and the penalties for early surrenders are steep. Federal tax penalties also kick in if annuities are redeemed before their owners reach age 59. If you put money into an annuity, you're pretty much locking it up for some time.

Variable annuities

Years ago, insurance companies wanted to get a piece of the investment pie, so they successfully lobbied Congress to allow them to sell tax-deferred investment products called variable annuities. Variable annuities allow investors to invest in separate accounts that are similar to mutual funds. Each type of investment has varying risks and returns. An insurance component guarantees that when the investor dies, his or her beneficiaries will receive at least what the investor put in. The earnings from variable annuities—dividends, interest, and growth—are not taxed until the investor cashes them in.

Insurance companies that manage variable annuities keep their annuity funds in separate accounts, not in their general funds. Because variable annuity funds are not mixed with the insurance company's assets, they are not at risk if the insurance company fails.

Fixed annuities

Another type of annuity is fixed annuities, which are interest-bearing annuities. They are safer than variable annuities, because their prices don't fluctuate. Fixed annuities stay the same and just pay interest. The big risk is that if you want to take your money out early, you must pay costly penalties.

Another drawback with fixed annuity funds is that they are mixed with the insurance companies' general assets. That includes cash-value insurance funds, which are moneys that build up in cash-value life insurance policies. So if the insurance company fails, fixed annuity owners are general creditors, who at best would only receive a portion of every dollar they invested.

Until recently, insurance companies were one of the safest places for investors' money. However, because they invested much of the funds they received from selling fixed annuities in bonds, mortgages, and commercial real estate loans, all of which are now tanking, most insurance companies are losing lots of money and their stocks are plummeting. In fact, a number of large insurance companies have received bailout money from the federal government to keep them afloat.

I don't like either variable or fixed annuities. Because they pay financial advisors the highest commissions of any of the basic investments, they are highly touted. Despite the conflict of interest, many financial advisors only sell annuities because they pay the highest commission, not because they are in their clients' best interests.

TREATMENT

Save 10 percent of your gross income. That amount can include your contributions to retirement programs, such as 401(k) plans. Savings is the first place to put money. *If you don't have enough in savings you should not invest.*

How much is enough savings? If you lose your job or can't work, you need to have enough money in your savings account to see you through. Naturally, that amount will vary with each individual and his or her unique circumstances. Some financial planners recommend amassing enough savings to last six months. I think it should be more than that. Money has a way of vanishing sooner than we expect, getting new jobs can take time, and emergencies and unexpected expenses always tend to crop up. Accumulate enough savings to last up to one year. If you're secure in your employment, are self-employed, or have little chance of losing your job, saving enough to carry you for six to nine months should be fine. If you have a more specialized career that has limited employment opportunities, your emergency fund should be for no less than one year. Having money saved for one year will give you plenty of time to look for a job without having to worry about how you're going to pay your mortgage and feed your kids.

When you've built a sufficient amount of savings, invest. This chapter is only an introduction. Learn more about investing so you can do so wisely. As discussed in the previous chapter, find a financial advisor whom you trust to help you develop a plan.

My Rx

Regularly monitor the performance of your investments because, at times, you will need to make adjustments. During recessions or market declines, think about lowering the percentage of the money you have invested in equity-oriented mutual funds and increasing the amount when the economy is starting to turn.

Also, as you grow older, decrease the amount of money you have in the stock market. Ralph and Helen, both in their late 70s, recently came to see me for the first time. They had put more than 80 percent of their money in stock market–oriented investments. When the market crashed, they lost 40 percent of their retirement nest egg. Poor asset allocation threw their financial health into critical condition.

The formula frequently used for risk tolerance recommends subtracting your age from 100, which leaves you with the maximum amount of your money that should be in stock market–oriented investments. For instance, if you're 35, invest no more than 65 percent of your money in stock market–oriented investments. If you're 70, invest no more than 30 percent of your money in stock market–oriented investments. The reasoning is that as you grow older, you should be more conservative, reducing your risk and becoming more income-oriented, because you have less time to rebuild any losses you might sustain. If you're 35 and have most of your money invested in the stock market, it's generally not a big problem if the stock market goes down. You have plenty of time to make it back. Because you're building assets for the future, you can afford to be patient, as the stock market has historically come back. If you're 65 and heavily invested in the stock market, it could be a big problem, because you probably won't have enough time to make your losses back. You don't want to be in the same position as many seniors who recently saw their retirement plans destroyed because they had invested too much of their money in the stock market.

Chapter 10
Failing to Diversify Investments

The Ailment

Investment disasters occur frequently because of lack of diversification. Countless investors have lost all their money because they didn't diversify their investments. These poor souls put all their money into too few investments, and, when those investments went south, they were wiped out.

Many workers invested all their retirement savings in their employers' stock. When their companies went under, the employees' retirement funds were virtually worthless. Not only did those workers lose their jobs, but their futures were also destroyed.

The key to successful investing is to not take substantial losses, because big losses are hard to recoup. If you suffer a 50 percent loss, you need a 100 percent return just to get even. Diversification makes devastating losses virtually impossible.

Diagnosis

No one is totally immune from the temptation to put all their eggs in a potentially profitable basket. When certain investments show great promise, even savvy investors are drawn in; they become greedy and go overboard. Instead of investing conservatively, they throw caution to the wind and take great risks. They invest large sums of money in an individual stock, a single real estate deal, or a lone business venture, in order to reap big rewards.

Some investors deliberately put everything they have into one investment in order to catch up, especially if they have not invested or built much wealth, or they may have suffered big losses that they hope to recoup. They want to make a fortune in one grand swoop, so they plunk down everything and go for broke—and that's what frequently happens.

Investors who work for publicly traded corporations often tend to be myopic. They believe in their companies, hear about developments that the brass touts, and buy into all the company rah-rah. They know what is in the company pipeline and put everything on the line, because they think of themselves as insiders who have special information and insights.

In reality, employees rarely know all the facts. They usually hear just bits and pieces, not the whole story, and are not privy to decisions and problems that may determine the fate of their companies. How many people who worked for World Com, Lucent, and General Motors knew the entire picture? If they had, would they have kept all their retirement savings in the shares of these huge, multinational corporations, which then collapsed?

Vital Signs

Diversification comes in a number of forms. The most common are asset diversification, specific company diversification, and sector diversification.

Asset diversification refers to the various types of assets you own—holding different types of assets such as stocks, bonds, real estate, and bank savings. When you invest, your objective should be to balance your holdings, to spread your money among a number of different types of investments to reduce your risks.

Specific company or investment-type diversification occurs within asset groups. For securities, it would be investing in a number of different companies' stocks or utilizing diversified mutual funds. For bonds, it's the ownership of different types of federal government or municipal bonds. In real estate, it's different types of property such as residential, commercial, or vacant land. As I mentioned, the failure to diversify among specific company securities has taken a huge toll. If you had worked for Circuit City and had all your 401(k) savings in the company stock, you would have lost virtually all that money when Circuit City went out of business. Unfortunately, this scenario repeatedly occurred when many major corporations failed.

Sector diversification is having investments in more than one trade sector. Having all your investments in a certain field, such as technology, finance, or healthcare, concentrates your risk. Entire sectors of the economy have their ups and downs, so the stocks in those industries will rise and fall with the sector. Many people got burned when technology stocks crashed in 2000, because they held too much stock in that sector. If you concentrate your stock purchases or own mutual funds or ETFs that deal exclusively in a specific sector, you can be at risk. Again, your best bet is to balance your investments in different sectors.

The following pie charts illustrate the recommended allocation of assets for people age 30, 50, 65, and 75, excluding real estate.

Asset Allocation - Age 30

Proper asset allocations for 30-year-olds.

Asset Allocation - Age 50

Proper asset allocation for 50-year-olds.

Asset Allocation - Age 65

Proper asset allocation for 65-year-olds.

Asset Allocation - Age 75

Proper asset allocation for 75-year-olds.

TREATMENT

Diversify; spread your investments around. I always advise my clients and radio audience to buy mutual funds, because the diversification they provide decreases your risk and gives you more safety.

As you build your portfolio, think beyond the usual stocks, bonds, and savings. Although those assets definitely should be a part of your holdings, think about investing in other areas.

Consider investing in real estate. Owning your home has always been an excellent investment and provides great tax benefits. Although the real estate market is now in a major slump, in the long term, real estate keeps pace with inflation. Watch out for speculative real estate ventures. They can be risky and have ruined many investors.

Collectables, including art, jewelry, coins, stamps, and antiques, when carefully chosen, usually keep pace with inflation.

ETFs make it easy to invest in tangible assets such as oil and agricultural commodities.

Historically, precious metals have been a good hedge against inflation. Investments in gold and silver have traditionally risen in periods of recession and bad economic times. Think about investing 5 to 10 percent of your assets in precious metals.

Putting money into your business can also be an excellent investment. However, many people put everything into their businesses and have little or no other investments. Although keeping your business productive and profitable is a must, it also may entail risk, especially if you're in a highly competitive business sector. Calculate the return you're getting from investing in your business and compare it with what you could earn from other investments. If too much of your money is tied up in your business, move some of it into other investments, or see if you can get reasonably priced financing or partners who are willing to invest in your business. If you decide to invest, try to find liquid investments so you can have access to your funds should you need them for your business.

My Rx

As I mentioned at the beginning of this chapter, even the most savvy of investors are susceptible to going for broke. In 1996, I found out about Crystallex International, a small, publicly traded gold exploration company with projects in Venezuela. Crystallex had recently acquired a small Venezuelan company that claimed to have the rights to Las Cristinas, a gigantic 9-million-ounce gold mine being developed by a large, international mining company. Crystallex went to court in Venezuela, claiming that it had the rights to the mine. If it succeeded, Crystallex's stock would soar, and its shareholders would get rich.

I invested about 80 percent of my savings in Crystallex and told my friends, family, and clients to buy as much as they could. In the months before the court's decision, the stock rose from $1.20 a share to more than $6. We were all making lots of money—on paper. If Crystallex prevailed, as seemed likely, the stock would have shot to more than $20. However, in June 1998, the Venezuelan Supreme Court ruled against Crystallex (in what is widely considered a corrupt verdict), and the stock crashed to 35 cents. I lost most of my savings and that of my friends, family, and clients. It was a day I will never forget! I learned my lesson the expensive way. Diversify; never bet the farm on any one investment.

If you decide to invest, hedge your bets by not risking everything you own. The best, most foolproof, can't-miss investments can bomb. The most trusted, reliable tips may not pan out, so use restraint and don't put all of your money in one place. Be happy making smaller profits and live to fight another day.

Although well-diversified portfolios can decline in value during bad markets, they rarely incur severe, financial goal damaging losses.

Remember: the concept of building net worth is based on not losing what you have worked so hard to build through the years.

CHAPTER 11
NOT UNDERSTANDING THE IMPACT OF INFLATION

THE AILMENT

Inflation is a slow-moving disease in the financial body that erodes our purchasing power. Inflation occurs when the money supply expands. When more money is in circulation, it dilutes how much our dollars can buy. Assets, goods, and services rise in price. Here's an example of how it works.

On July 1, 2008, Jack bought $100 worth of goods, and he also purchased a Certificate of Deposit for $100 that paid 4-percent interest. A year later, Jack cashed in the CD and received $104. However, Uncle Sam took $1 of Jack's earnings for taxes, so Jack had only $103 to spend. If the rate of inflation was 5 percent, it would cost Jack $105 to buy all the same items he bought on July 1, 2008. Factoring in taxes and the rate of inflation, Jack's buying power decreased by 2 percent in one year.

Deflation is the flip side of inflation. It occurs when the money supply contracts. When less money is available, prices drop virtually across the board. However, the amount of your debt stays the same. When the value of your home decreases, your mortgage debt stays the same. Your mortgage payments don't go down, but your equity declines. When compared to your other costs, your debt is magnified. And while your debt magnifies, so does corporate and government debt.

Governments prefer inflation to deflation. In financial crises, they historically print money even though they know that their weakened currency will buy less. Prepare yourself; be ready to go through a period of slow-rising inflation and invest in inflation-proof assets.

DIAGNOSIS

Inflation is the enemy of building wealth, because it reduces the value of what you earn. Inflation forces you to swim against the tide. Like strong currents, inflation can exhaust you and your money and may drag you under.

Inflation is insidious because it sneaks up on us. Because it tends to advance in small increments, we don't immediately feel its affect. Then, sometime later, we realize that everything we buy is costing more.

Another hidden fact about inflation is that it compounds. As inflation compounds, your purchasing power weakens. In time, the amount of those losses can be substantial.

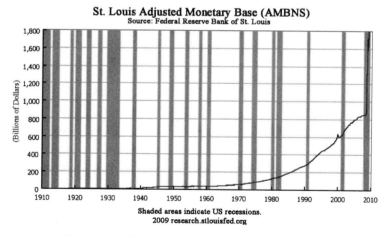

Increased U.S. Money Supply from 1910 to 2009

Look at the dramatic rise in the money supply in the last two years; it's staggering!

Governments monitor inflation closely and try to manage it, because it can destabilize their economies. In response to the present financial crises, the U.S. Federal Reserve Board essentially printed money to finance our deficits and the corporate bailouts. Because so much money was injected into the system, we can expect higher inflation in the future. Therefore, when we manage our money in order to build wealth, we must take inflation into account, because tomorrow our dollars won't buy as much as they buy today.

VITAL SIGNS

Inflation can spread like wildfire. It may start slowly, but can quickly erupt out of control and be hard to stop. When inflation kicks up, expectations fan its flames. They have as great an effect as the rising prices themselves. If people know that in six months, a product will be more expensive, they will rush out to buy as much of it as they can. Suddenly, the demand for the item will shoot up and the supply will drop. In other words, expectations of inflation become reality when products are in short supply. As the prices for those products increase, inflation soars.

Each month, the U.S. Bureau of Labor Statistics (*www.bls.gov/ cpi*) publishes the Consumer Price Index (CPI), which lists the current rate of inflation. The CPI is not always an accurate gauge of inflation, because the government has been known to make inflation seem to be lower than it actually is. It's in the government's interests to make inflation seem low in order to boost confidence in the economy, and because social security and other government entitlement programs have cost-of-living adjustments tied to the CPI. The real rate of inflation is at least two to three percentage points greater than the government reports.

If all your money is deposited in savings accounts, that money will be safe and secure, but you will be eaten alive by inflation, because your purchasing power will be steadily drained. When all your money is in the bank, I call it "going broke safely," because every year your money buys less.

Although savings should be a part of your overall financial picture, placing all of your money in savings alone is not wise because the interest you earn will usually be less than taxes and the rate of inflation. Too many people have retired and thought that they were in good financial shape because they had built nice nest eggs and were receiving pension and social security payments. Then, inflation nibbled away at their purchasing power, prices rose, and making ends meet in retirement became a struggle.

TREATMENT

There are several moves you can make to safeguard your wealth against inflation.

Adjust your portfolio

Make preserving your purchasing power your number-one goal. Focus on the real rate of return on your money (the amount of return on your investments, minus taxes and the rate of inflation). Adjust your portfolio to make sure that your real of return stays in positive territory.

Put your money in investments that traditionally return more than the rate of inflation. Although those investments may expose you to greater risk than deposits in your bank account would, diversification and the proper asset allocation will minimize your risk.

During inflation

Except for bonds and money deposited in savings accounts, virtually all other investments have historically kept pace with inflation. Inflation-beating investments will fluctuate from time to time, but, in the long term, your returns should exceed the rate of inflation. Buy tangible investments such as commodities, oil, precious metals, real estate, stocks, and mutual funds that own stock, because they tend to perform well during inflationary periods.

The following are investments that do well in periods of inflation. They are listed in order of how well they have traditionally performed.

1. Precious Metals. Buying gold and silver has historically been the number-one hedge against inflation. Just 50 years ago, one ounce of gold could buy a good-quality man's suit, and the same holds true today. Gold recently traded for more than $1,000 an ounce, because of fears that the government's injection of dollars into the economy to fund the deficit would cause inflation. Gold and silver can be bought in coins, in publicly traded funds, or by investing in mining companies.

2. Commodities. Commodities are items that we consume everyday. Commodities such as food and energy rise during periods of inflation, so buying shares of companies involved in the production and/or distribution of commodities will enable you to keep pace. Because many mutual funds and ETFs invest in these companies, it is now easy for investors to get into the commodity market.

3. Treasury Inflation Protected Securities (TIPS). TIPS principle value is adjusted according to changes in the CPI: they rise with inflation and falls with deflation. Traditional Treasury securities fall in value during periods of inflation and rise during periods of deflation, which makes TIPS a better investment during inflationary periods. You can buy publicly traded ETFs such as iShares Barclays TIPS Bond. You can buy TIPS directly from the U.S. Treasury or invest in

mutual funds such as Vanguard Inflation-Protected Securities.

4. I-Bonds. I-Bonds are savings bonds issued by the U.S. government that are inflation-indexed. They have two components: a fixed interest rate that remains for the life of the bond, and an inflation-adjusted variable rate. Every six months (May 1 and November 1), the interest rate is adjusted based on changes in the CPI. During periods of high inflation, I-Bond owners are compensated with a higher interest rate. The drawback of I-Bonds is that each purchaser can buy only $10,000 worth per year, $5,000 in paper bonds and $5,000 purchased online from the U.S. Treasury.

5. High Dividend Paying Stocks. During inflationary periods, the dividend yield for stocks on the S&P 500 has historically been quite close to the rate of inflation. Stocks also tend to rise in value during times of inflation. You can purchase stocks that pay high dividends individually and build a diversified portfolio, or, better yet, buy an S&P 500 index fund, such as the Vanguard S&P 500 Investors Shares mutual fund.

During deflation

Periods of deflation are far less common than periods of inflation, but occur during severe economic contraction, such as the recent financial crisis. Asset prices decline when no one wants to spend money. Stock prices, real estate, and commodities all decline when the economy is hurting.

Following are the top investments for periods of deflation.

1. 30-Year U.S. Treasury Bonds. During deflationary periods, bonds with long maturity terms tend to perform better than other investment alternatives. They are a safe alternative to investments in depreciating assets

such as stocks and real estate. In times of deflation, investors become more risk averse, sell stocks, and move to the safety of U.S. Treasury Bonds. The Federal Reserve lowers interest rates during deflationary periods, which results in rising Treasury Bond prices. U.S. 30-year bonds usually pay higher interest rates than bonds that mature sooner. You can buy 30-year bonds directly from the U.S. Treasury, from a broker, or by investing in mutual funds and exchange traded funds that hold long-maturity bonds.

2. Gold. Why is gold on both the inflation and deflation list? Gold tends to perform well during both inflationary and deflation periods. Investors buy gold as a safe haven in time of financial instability and uncertainty. During the recent financial crisis, the price of gold actually rose because investors lost confidence in the stock market, banks, and other financial institutions.

3. Paying Off Debt. Paying off your debt is not an investment, but it makes sense to eliminate as much debt as possible during a deflationary period. Debt becomes more burdensome during periods when asset prices are falling. Everyone has less money to spend, which makes paying off debt more difficult. Being debt-free is advisable in any economic environment and can help you survive the tough economic times that accompany deflation.

Active management

Don't be a passive investor. Work with financial advisors who are active money managers, build close working relationships with your financial advisors, learn about investments, regularly monitor your investments, and be involved in the management of your money.

Many investors do business with commissioned brokers who put them into investments and then turn their focus to other clients. Brokers are salespeople, not money managers. As soon as they earn a commission, they forget about you and move on to other clients who will pay them more commissions.

Most brokers don't monitor their clients' accounts to see whether their clients' earnings are exceeding the rate of inflation. They don't act to protect their clients or recommend necessary changes in their portfolios. In the past year, millions of Americans lost 40 to 50 percent of their nest eggs because they were passive investors and their brokers didn't properly manage their money.

In 2008, my firm's financial-planning actively managed accounts didn't lose a dime on their investments, because we moved 100 percent of their money into money-market funds when it became evident that the financial crisis had begun. We saw the breakdown of the financial system and the defaults in subprime mortgages, and put their money where it was safe. It wasn't brilliance on our part, but it was diligence. We kept our eyes open, paid attention, and actively managed our clients' money.

My Rx

In the last year, we witnessed deflation in real estate and stock prices, but, in the future, prices will rapidly rise for everything. For decades, the prices of goods and services have continually increased and the explosive expansion of the money supply will result in higher inflation in the years to come. Be sure to make investments that will perform well in an inflationary environment.

The current financial crisis has changed the financial landscape. The huge financial losses that so many investors suffered have become a mandate for change. If you haven't become an active, engaged investor, start now or you may wind up in financial intensive care.

Passive investing no longer works. The traditional buy-and-hold strategy that enabled investors to build fortunes has had its day. Now, investors must be actively engaged in their money and with their financial team. They must position themselves to both make profits and quickly get out of markets that are not performing well.

If your financial advisor is a commissioned salesperson who doesn't actively manage your account, think about replacing him or her with an advisor who will actively manage your funds and who works on a fee basis.

Chapter 12
Failing to Use the Tax Code to Your Advantage

The Ailment

The federal government is our partner in all our financial ventures: we do all the work, but it takes a cut of everything we earn! However, the government also gives us many opportunities to avoid, reduce, or defer taxes, but many people don't take advantage of them. They pay more taxes than necessary, because they don't know the law or get professional tax advice.

I call taxes "financial side effects." Just as every medication has its side effects, every financial transaction has tax consequences. If you want to boost your financial health, learn how to save money by paying as little taxes as possible.

Diagnosis

Ignorance is the number-one reason why taxpayers pay too much in taxes. They don't know what benefits they are entitled to and how to use the tax code to their advantage—and it costs them money.

The second reason is closely associated with the first; it's the failure of taxpayers to get good tax advice. Our tax laws are detailed and complex. We have to pay a number of taxes—federal, state, and local. In addition, our laws and regulations in each of these areas are always changing and being reinterpreted.

Although taxes affect all of us, most of us have little or no knowledge or understanding of them. We don't have time to keep up with all the tax information that applies to us, and even if we did, most of us wouldn't fully understand the implications. Despite that fact, we don't work with experts in taxes and finance, so we end up paying more than we're required to pay.

VITAL SIGNS

Our tax laws are complex, but I'm going to give you an introduction to some of the savings that could be available to you. Although you probably already know some, others may be new to you. See if any of them apply to you, and, if so, learn more about them. Become familiar with the terms and general approach. Then meet with a financial advisor or tax professional to examine how particular areas could benefit you.

Capital gains

When you sell a capital asset that you've held for at least one year, you are entitled to long-term capital gains treatment. The profit or loss from that sale is subject to capital gains tax, which is now a maximum of 15 percent. (However, President Obama's 2010 budget proposal calls for higher capital gains rates.) If you sell a capital asset that you've owned for less than one year, you receive short-term capital gains treatment and must pay taxes at your ordinary income rate, which is usually substantially more than 15 percent. Capital assets include a wide variety of investments including stocks, bonds, mutual funds, collectibles, real estate, and businesses.

Tax incentives

From time to time, the U.S. government makes it worthwhile for taxpayers to make certain expenditures. Notable tax incentives have been given to taxpayers for the cost of higher education, to buy environmentally friendly cars, and to improve the energy efficiency of their homes and workplaces.

Recently, Uncle Sam offered an $8,000 first-time home buyer credit (if buyers have not bought a home in three years), which is a dollar-for-dollar refundable credit.

Retirement plans

The most common retirement plans are tax-deferred vehicles such as traditional individual retirement accounts (IRAs), 401(k) plans, and pension accounts. 403(b) plans are virtually the same as 401(k) plans, but are for hospital, school and university, civil government, and not-for-profit corporation employees.

You can contribute a portion of your salary to a retirement plan and defer taxes on the growth of those funds until they are withdrawn. However, the government has placed limits on the amounts you can contribute.

Many retirement plans allow you to borrow from them under certain circumstances. In most cases, funds cannot be withdrawn until plan owners are 59 and a half years old. If withdrawals are made sooner, steep tax penalties are imposed. Loans may be made from most retirement plan funds. The following are brief descriptions of the most popular plans.

Individual retirement accounts

A traditional IRA allows:

☑ Individuals to contribute up to $5,000 each year to a tax-deferred retirement account.

☑ Individuals 50 years of age and older to put in up to $6,000 annually.

☑ Couples can annually contribute up to $10,000 or $12,000 if both are 50 or older.

Traditional IRAs have two advantages: First, you can deduct the amount you contribute from your income taxes in the year of your contribution. So if you're in a high tax bracket today, by putting money into an IRA you'll get a significant tax savings. Second, all profits, such as dividends and interest, are tax deferred, so you don't pay any taxes on them until you take the money out. In the majority of cases, when you take the money out, you're in a lower tax bracket, so you enjoy additional savings. Also, you don't have to pay taxes on the money you earn, so you can reinvest it and let it compound, which enables you to make much more money.

When large withdrawals are made from IRA plans, the receipt of those funds can put taxpayers in higher brackets. It can also cause taxpayers' Social Security payments to be taxed.

Taxpayers with IRAs must take minimum distributions when they reach the age of 70 and a half years old. Those distributions are taxable in the tax year when they distributed. If you have a Roth IRA, you are not required to take distributions. If you do take distributions, they are tax free if you are over the age of 59 and a half years old.

401(k) plans

As of 2009, employees can contribute as much as $16,500 of their salaries to 401(k) plans. Those who are 50 or older can put in as much as $22,000. If you're an employee, payments to your 401(k) are taken out of your pre-tax paycheck. Employers put your payments directly into your 401(k) account, along with the amounts they match, if any. You can invest your 401(k) funds in a number of investment vehicles and, similar to IRAs, the earnings from your 401(k) plan are tax deferred until the time you withdraw money from your account.

When money comes out of each paycheck and is put in a 401(k) account, you are dollar-cost averaging your investments. That means that you are purchasing those investments at varying values, but you are buying them on a consistent basis. When markets are depressed, dollar-cost averaging works to your advantage, because you can buy new investments at lower prices.

With a 401(k) plan, you don't have to worry about saving money, because your employer automatically does it for you. Your plan is also a forced, but painless, way of saving, because funds are taken directly out of your pre-tax paycheck. Most people quickly adjust to their reduced take-home pay and never miss the money that goes into their 401(k) plans. If your 401(k) plan includes a company match, put in the maximum your employer will match. Whatever your employer kicks in is free money, and it gives you immediate returns.

Roth IRAs and 401(k) plans

Your contributions to Roth plans are not tax deductible, but these plans have become popular because you don't have to pay taxes on the money you withdraw after you reach the age of 59 and a half years old. Many people are willing to pay a small amount of taxes when they make their Roth contributions in order to get tax-free distributions when they retire.

Pension plans

Companies traditionally gave their employees defined benefit plans or pensions, which they paid when employees retired. For most companies, those plans are now history and no longer a part of employees' benefit packages. Now, employees' 401(k) plans represent their entire retirement funds. Pensions have been replaced by defined contribution plans in which employees pay into their own 401(k) plans.

Municipal bonds

As I've previously mentioned, municipal bonds are loans to states, cities, and other state and local governmental units. The interest is not federally taxable and is tax-free for residents of the states that issued the bonds. Traditionally, municipal bonds were considered a safe investment, but, during the recent financial downturn, the risk of municipal bond defaults has increased. More defaults may occur because the revenues from state sales taxes, state income taxes, and local property taxes are down, resulting in skyrocketing budget deficits. States are financially shaky, and many of their pension funds are tremendously underfunded.

Reduce the risk of municipal bond defaults by investing in mutual funds that deal exclusively in municipal bonds. These funds receive interest from the bonds in their portfolios, and they typically pay fund owners a monthly dividend. Because municipal bond funds are well diversified—they own hundreds of different municipal bonds—you don't have to worry if any one issue defaults.

Some municipal bond mutual funds are state-specific; the income is tax-free to residents of those states. However, those funds are a bit more risky, because your investment is all in one state's economy.

In these uncertain economic times, I prefer to invest in national municipal bond funds that deal in bonds from many states. I like their diversification and am willing to forego the state tax exemption for the extra safety they provide. In most cases, the state taxes you have to pay are small, only a fraction of what you pay in federal taxes.

The higher your tax bracket, the more valuable municipal bonds can be for you. Concerns in the municipal bond market have caused prices to drop so their yields are now quite substantial when you compare them with other taxable investments. Typically, municipal bonds yield less than long-term, taxable U.S. Treasury bonds, but they are now yielding more.

Many municipal bonds are insured against default. However, the companies that insure these bonds are also going through financial difficulties. Don't get lured into buying municipal bonds because they're insured, because these companies may not be able to pay policyholders if massive municipal bond defaults occurred.

Annuities

Annuities, which I discussed in Chapter 9, also provide tax benefits. The tax on the income earned during the annuity term is deferred until the annuity is cashed in. As I pointed out, I don't like annuities and think that most people should avoid buying them— especially senior citizens, who are the largest market for annuities. In most cases, IRA accounts should not be invested in annuities, because IRAs are already tax-deferred vehicles.

I also believe that annuities should be standardized and subjected to more regulation. Particular attention should be focused on their management costs, redemption fee schedules, sales practices, and fee commissions.

TREATMENT

Keep up with the tax incentives the government offers. They can provide you with substantial savings. Consider it a part of your ongoing financial education and responsibility.

Plan and prepare for your taxes. Many people have little knowledge about taxes and do no tax planning or preparation, including those who run their own businesses. Everything taxpayers earn results in major tax consequences, which can be expensive. We all have to pay federal income taxes, and those who are self-employed must also pay self-employment taxes, which amount to roughly 17 percent more than the taxpayer's ordinary income tax rate, in addition to any state and local taxes due.

Because self-employed people don't have taxes withheld, they can get into tax trouble. If they don't plan, put money aside, and make quarterly estimated tax payments, they can be hit big on April 15. If they can't pay all the taxes they owe the government on time, penalties and interest will be added.

When combined, paying all this money can derail a fledgling business. Although it's sometimes difficult to plan and set aside money for taxes, the alternative is worse. The obligation to pay taxes is not wiped out by bankruptcy and can take years to pay. In the meantime, it becomes a big red flag that will ruin your credit and make it hard to get back on your feet.

Work with a tax professional. Put a good tax accountant, advisor, or preparer on your financial team, especially if you have your own business! Our tax laws—federal, state, and local—are detailed, and complex. They are always being interpreted and changed, so it's hard to keep up. Changes can easily slip by you and cause you to miss out on sizable tax savings.

Too many people try to do their own taxes and manage their financial affairs without expert help. Good tax professional are experts who know the ropes. Unlike you, they specialize in and have experience with a wide range of tax situations. Like all experts, tax professionals are up on the latest laws, rules, and regulations. They know the recent changes and interpretations and can give you invaluable advice on all sorts of financial and business matters. The fees you pay for professional tax services are wise investments that can help you build your wealth.

MY Rx

Though tax evasion is illegal, paying the least taxes possible should be the goal of everyone who wants to build wealth. Because the government has established ways for us to defer, lower, or avoid taxes on our income, it's important to take advantage of them, especially if you are in a high tax bracket. Work hard, earn money, and use every legal means possible to keep as much as you can.

Take advantage of tax-free and tax-deferred investments. Our taxes are already increasing and further increases are inevitable, because the federal and state governments need more of our money to address huge budget deficits and shortfalls.

Don't let that fact that you will incur taxes prevent you from selling an investment. Some of my clients decided not to sell investments because of the tax consequences, but many of them lost more money by hanging onto those investments.

Every financial move you make has tax implications, so before entering into any transaction, consider how your taxes will be affected!

Remember: tax evasion is illegal, but legal tax avoidance is your right. If you want to build wealth, you must do whatever you legally can to keep your tax bills to a minimum.

CHAPTER 13
BUYING TOO
MUCH HOUSE

THE AILMENT

Once you buy a home, your expenses increase, often soaring dramatically if you buy a large, costly house. When you become a homeowner, you're no longer paying just the monthly rent and a few incidentals. Instead, all sorts of new expenses crop up; before long, they all increase. In addition to mortgage payments, you have property taxes, insurance, utilities, upkeep, maintenance, and perhaps assessments. Add on the costs of furnishings, repairs, renovations, remodeling, and a stream of other expenses. It all mounts up.

Buying too much home can decrease your savings and deplete your investments. It can also cut into how much you have left to save, invest, and use to enjoy other aspects of your life, including your home.

DIAGNOSIS

Purchasing and financing a home is most families' costliest, longest-term obligation. Getting into a home frequently wipes out their savings and investments, or at least a good portion of them. Moreover, their monthly mortgage payments can eat up the bulk of their income, which decreases the amount of money they have to save and invest.

Recently, it was easy to get mortgages, so people were lured into buying larger and more expensive homes than they needed or could afford. Lenders didn't require large or, in many cases, any down payments. As a result, buyers initially had low monthly mortgage payments. However, those payments rose after a certain period of time, and the increases were often substantial and more than borrowers could pay.

When their higher interest rates kicked in, millions of home-owners couldn't pay their monthly mortgage payments, so they lost their homes and destroyed their credit. The impact was so wide-spread that it created the global financial crisis that is expected to haunt us for years.

VITAL SIGNS

Today, many people feel a sense of entitlement; they are ego-driven, status-conscious, and determined to lead glamorous lives. They believe that they have the right to live luxuriously, so they buy homes that are beyond their means and needs. To boost their egos and impress others, they want castles, show places, McMansions with all the trimmings. Their huge houses must include great rooms, deluxe kitchens, swimming pools, exotic landscaping, decks, finished basements, and all the latest gadgets. Of course, they need the appropriate cars, clothes, furnishings, vacations, and activities to go with them.

In the past, families were more rooted and remained in the same homes for years. Many raised their children and lived in the same house until they retired. Now, more families are quicker to move and are continually looking to trade up. In the course of their lives, they buy a number of homes that are progressively larger and more expensive. Those who stay put often refinance and take out home equity loans for additions and other improvements.

Having larger, more expensive homes forces homeowners to devote a higher percentage of their income to their dwellings. Because property taxes and insurance are based on the value of the home, they cost more, as do maintenance and utility expenses. In most cases, their expenses ratchet up so they have less money to save and invest. As a result, the average American family saves little, owes more, and lives from paycheck to paycheck.

In recent years, people have been buying and financing homes without putting down much or any money. Traditionally, buyers were required to put 20 percent down, because banks wouldn't lend more than 80 percent of the value of the home. But in the 1990s, that all changed, and those changes had unintended consequences—they triggered the present financial crisis.

TREATMENT

A house is a place to live. First and foremost, it should be a comfortable residence for you and your family, not something intended to wow the world. If you have children, your home should be a safe, secure, and comfortable place for them to grow. A house does not have to be a castle, a showcase, or a balm for the owner's ego.

What to do

Hold off buying a home until you can put 20 percent down. When trouble arises, people who don't make a substantial down payment are more likely to walk away, because they have little or nothing invested. However, walking away will ruin their credit, which they may never be able to restore.

If you put down 20 percent, it gives you a cushion. If the market goes down, you still have equity in your home. And, in time, the value of your home will probably appreciate, and your 20 percent will become 30 percent, 40 percent, and so on. For millions of people, the equity growth in their home has been their main savings; it has given them the funds to enjoy comfortable retirement lives.

Scale down. Instead of purchasing a big or expensive home, take a more modest, smaller approach. First, understand your income, expenses, and asset structure, so you can buy a home that you can afford. You don't want a home that will financially squeeze you, but one that will leave you with enough money to enjoy your life, and to save and invest for your future.

Investigate fully before you buy. Look into the neighborhood and consider how its character could change. Anticipate future expenses and make provisions for them. Be prepared for property tax increases, the possibility of assessments, and increased costs in insurance, utilities, and other expenses.

When buying a home, only take a 15- or 30-year fixed-rate mortgage. The beauty of fixed-rate mortgages is that they are simple to understand, and the lender can't change the terms of the loan. Although your property taxes can increase, the increases are usually reasonable, and you can still build the equity in your home. Then, if somewhere down the road you need funds, you can take out a home equity loan (although I hope it can be avoided) or refinance at a lower interest rate.

Understand your mortgage before you sign on. Mortgages can be complicated and you have the right to have yours fully explained. Make sure that you understand all the details—especially your obligations. Specifically, know:

- ☑ The mortgage term.
- ☑ The interest rate throughout the term.
- ☑ All costs and fees you will have to pay to get or refinance the mortgage.
- ☑ The amount to which, and exactly when, interest rates reset, if they do.
- ☑ How the new interest rate will be calculated.

☑ Whether the mortgage includes a prepayment penalty and, if so, for how long and how much.

☑ If qualified individuals can assume your mortgage obligation.

What not to do

Don't buy a home unless you can make a substantial down payment, something in the area of 20 percent. If you can't put down 20 percent and afford the monthly payments for a 30-year, fixed-payment mortgage, you're not ready to buy a home. Wait, save, build up more, buy a less expensive home, or simply rent, which is not such a bad option in a falling housing market. Don't strangle yourself financially, because you'll regret it.

Under no circumstances should you take out an interest-only mortgage, because you will not be able to build equity or pay down the principle. Worse yet are negative amortization mortgages (option ARMs), which operate like credit cards and allow you to make minimum payments. Those minimum payments frequently don't cover the mortgage interest, so instead of paying down your debt, you're constantly taking on more.

Avoid adjustable rate mortgages. When you take an adjustable rate mortgage, you're gambling that mortgage interests rates will not increase in the future, which may be a very risky bet. The only time it makes sense to take an adjustable-rate mortgage is if the two following conditions are present: you get an initial low rate, and you know that will be selling your home before the expiration of that initial low-rate period.

Don't use your home as an ATM to constantly pull out cash. Build up equity. Traditionally, homes have been good, secure investments over the long term.

Questions to answer
before buying a home

Buying a home is a complex process that involves numerous, detailed steps, so it's easy to make mistakes. When you buy a home, it can wind up being a fabulous investment or a financial disaster. The choices you make are crucial, because they can affect you, your family, and your finances for many years.

Because every home and purchase differs, it's impossible to point out every step you should take. However, I want to highlight some major considerations that you shouldn't overlook. Before you begin the process of buying a home, answer the following questions:

What can you afford?

How much do you have to spend? How much can you put down and what amount will you have to borrow? The costs of buying a home fall into three major categories: the down payment, carrying costs, and closing costs. When you know the costs that will be involved in your purchase, the home-buying process will be easier, and you may be able to make a better deal. Take into consideration:

1. Down payment. Make a substantial down payment— no less than 20 percent of the purchase price. It will enable you to build equity in your home and give you a greater stake in your property. Consider it an investment, because historically real estate values rise in time and the value of your house will probably increase. The odds are that you'll more than get this one-time payment back. If you can't put down 20 percent of the purchase price, you can't afford the house—period!

    Multiply the amount you can have for a down payment by five. The figure you get will be the maximum that you should pay to buy a house. For example, if you have $40,000 for a down payment, you can afford a $200,000 home.

2. Carrying costs. This is the amount you have to pay each month, your total housing expenses. Essentially, your carrying costs consist of the principal and interest on your mortgage, real estate taxes, and insurance. Also include the costs of utilities such as gas, electricity, water, cable, and trash collection.

When lenders decide whether you qualify for a loan, they want assurances that you can pay your monthly mortgage payments. They will look to see if your total carrying costs do not exceed 28 percent of your gross monthly income. Remember that your housing expenses are recurrent costs that you must pay every month. For example, if your gross monthly income is $6,000 per month, 28 percent of $6,000 equals $1,680 per month. If your carrying costs are $450 a month, you could pay $1,230 for your monthly mortgage payment ($450 + $1,230 = $1,680). Based on those figures, you could qualify to borrow $246,000 on a 30-year fixed-rate mortgage at 6 percent. Therefore, you could afford to buy a home that costs no more than $307,500 if you made a $61,500 down payment.

Usually, salaries and earnings increase, so many buyers initially take on carrying costs that push them to their limits. They figure that they can bite the bullet until their incomes rise. In most cases, this approach works, but if a problem comes up before they make more money, they can be caught in a financial squeeze.

Play it safe; give yourself some room. Don't spend everything you earn on carrying costs for your home. Make sure to have some money left each month for price increases and unexpected expenses. As I'm sure you know, the price of virtually everything will go up, and price increases tend to come in bunches. And as a homeowner—especially if you have a family—unexpected expenses are a fact of life and most cost more than you were prepared to pay.

3. Closing costs. When you close title, your closing costs are the expenses that you will be required to pay in addition to the purchase price. Before you sign a contract to buy a home, ask your real estate agent or attorney for a written estimate of your closing costs, because they can add up. Although your agent or lawyer won't be able to give you the exact amount, they usually can come close.

Closing costs may include points, which is the percentage of the mortgage amount that a lender may demand to give you the loan. Each point is one percent of the mortgage amount. So if you agree to pay two points to get a mortgage for $180,000, you will have to pay $3,600 in points.

At the closing, you will also have to pay for items such as title searches, title insurance, a survey, recording fees, attorneys' fees, and escrows. Lenders usually require you to place money in escrow for at least six month's property taxes and your yearly insurance premium. Lenders can request more escrow funds when your taxes and insurance increase. Also be prepared to reimburse the seller for amounts he or she prepaid for utilities or other expenses you will use.

How good is your credit?

Before you go house hunting, find out how good your credit is, because it can determine whether or not you can get a mortgage and at what interest rate. Don't put yourself through the agony of falling in love with a house and then finding that you don't qualify for a large enough mortgage to buy it.

First, get a copy of your credit report at *www.annualcreditreport.com* or *www.freecreditreport.com*. You can get one free copy of your credit report each year. Also find out your FICO score, which may cost you a nominal fee.

FICO scores rate your credit and range from 300 to 850. Scores higher than 650 are good, but 700 or higher are better. If you have a higher FICO score, the interest rate you will be offered on a mortgage will be lower. If you have a poor score, hold off buying a house until you can improve your credit.

Get mortgage pre-approval. Pre-approval is a commitment by a lender to give you a mortgage up to a certain dollar amount. Pre-approval lets you know how much you can spend to purchase a home and shows real estate salespeople and sellers that you are a serious prospect who is qualified to buy.

What do you want?

Before you contact a real estate agent, draw up a list of the features you would like in your home. For example, the size of the property and house, the number of rooms and bathrooms, and the various features such as a finished basement, pool, garage, patio, yard, and landscaping. Also find out what local services are available and their costs, as well as the cost of utilities, cable, insurance, and property taxes.

Then find a real estate agent to represent you. Usually, the best way to find a good agent is by asking your friends and family. Question them about their experiences, what they liked and did not like, and then personally meet with and interview a few.

A good agent will help you find a home, negotiate the price, secure a mortgage, and advise you through the closing. It's important to hire an agent you like and trust, because you will be working very closely with him or her. It's also important that your agent be experienced and that he or she knows the area and is willing to spend as much time as is needed to find you exactly the home you want.

Inform your agent about your priorities. State which features you need in a home and those you would like. Make sure that you understand everything your agent tells you. Remember: your agent's job is to work for and represent you. He or she is supposed to do what is best for you, rather than what simply pleases the seller or closes the sale.

Where do you want to live?

They say that the most important consideration in buying real estate is location, location, location. Decide where you want to live; the options are virtually endless. What town, section, neighborhood, or street? You may want to live in an area in a top school district or a street with lots of families with children or near open space. You may want a home that is within walking distance of shopping, parks, or public transit. Do you need an area that is zoned for you to keep your horse?

Drive through neighborhoods and get a feel for them. See which ones you like and would be comfortable living in. Take note of the activity in the area, the way homes are maintained, and the number of homes for sale. If the turnover seems great, ask around to find the reasons.

Try to give yourself as many options as possible and don't limit yourself to one neighborhood. Listen to your real estate agent's suggestions. They are usually well informed and can show you areas you might not have known about or considered.

When you decide where you want to live, investigate the price range of homes in those areas. Check Websites that list homes in specific areas and their prices, such as *www.zillow.com*. You'll find that the nicer, more desirable areas are usually the most expensive.

What's the rush?

Because you're going to live in your home for many years, don't be impulsive and buy the first home that seems right—regardless of how hard your agent (or spouse) presses you. Plenty of homes are on the market, and new ones pop up every day. If you buy impulsively, you may regret it, and your haste can cost you much.

When my wife and I were looking to buy our first home, we found a lovely house the first weekend we began searching. In many ways, it wasn't quite right, but we were eager to own our own home and convinced ourselves that we could make it work. The more we thought about it, the more excited we became, so we made an offer. However, somebody beat us to it, and their offer was accepted before we bid.

We were heartbroken, crestfallen, crushed—but we continued to look. A few weeks later we found a terrific home, one that was much more suited to our needs. This one we really fell in love with. It had more land and potential, was in a nicer neighborhood, and was a much better deal. Now, after 15 years, we're still living in the same house and loving it even more.

What to offer?

It's usually not smart to agree to pay the listing price right off the bat. Sellers tend to initially set high sale prices, because they know that they will have to negotiate and come down. Most build wiggle room into their asking price.

If the real estate market is down, low bids are often accepted. If the real estate market is hot, sellers may get closer to the listing price, and they may even get more in areas where certain properties are in high demand.

If you find a house that you desperately want or a home that is in great demand, you may find yourself in a bidding war. If you really want the house, offer whatever you think it's worth—provided you can afford it. However, don't let your emotions carry you away. Always stay within your budget and buy only what you can afford.

If you pay a premium price, it can turn out to be a bargain, because you'll be happy in your home and in no rush to move. Moving can be an expensive and traumatic proposition. And because the value of most homes increases, the odds are that if you live there for a number of years, the premium you paid will be negligible or disappear in the long run—but your enjoyment and peace of mind will be well worth the price.

What is the property worth?

Before they give mortgage commitments, lenders must determine what the property is worth. They obtain an appraisal, which you will have to pay in advance. When you pay the appraisal fee, tell the lender that you want a copy of the appraisal and be sure to get one.

If the appraisal is lower than the price you agreed to pay for the house, discuss your options with your real estate agent. Frequently, sellers will lower the selling price rather than lose the sale, because they may not be able to find other buyers who will pay more than the appraised price.

How are contracts handled?

Congratulations! Your offer was accepted. Now it's time to sign a contract and give an earnest money deposit. Now, the legal formalities begin.

In some states, real estate agents collect deposits and handle the contracts. Agents usually work with title insurance companies that handle the searches, prepare all documents, and run the closings of title. In other states, each party—buyer and seller—hires a lawyer to represent them. The lawyers also work with title insurance companies, but the attorneys prepare all the paperwork and run the closings.

When your contract is prepared, make sure it details exactly what the sale includes. Are items such as furnishings, appliances, or outdoor equipment included in the sale? See to it that every item that is included in the sale is listed in the contract.

Any contingencies involved in the sale must be described clearly in the contract. The contract should state that your deposit will be refunded if specific contingencies cannot be met within a particular time. Contingencies that may be involved include obtaining a mortgage for a specified amount, selling your existing home or passing home, or termite or other inspections.

Specifically list in the contract all the reasons why the sale can be voided and your deposit money returned—for example, if you don't get a mortgage or the house doesn't pass an inspection. If the seller has the right to cure any of the contingencies, such as repairing termite damage, the contract should state the amount of time in which the cure must be made.

Make sure you fully understand *everything* in the contract. Don't sign it if it contains *anything* that you don't agree with or isn't clear to you—regardless of any promises you may receive. A written contract to buy a home is a binding legal document that can only be changed in writing, not by oral promises. If you have any doubts, consult a lawyer.

What is the home's condition?

Don't buy a home without having it inspected. Hire a competent, professional home inspector to examine the house for defects, termites, and other problems that occur in the area. If it's in a flood zone or rainy area, have it checked for water damage and/ or leaks.

Accompany the inspector during the inspection—it's a great way to learn about your new home. Some inspectors are chatty and will give you a running commentary about the pluses, minuses, and quality of the house, but others just want to be left alone to silently do their work. Most professional inspectors are very thorough. They will wend their way through crawl spaces and other areas that you may decide to skip.

If material defects or problems turn up, ask the seller to repair them, pay for the repairs, or lower the sales price. Be reasonable; homes are not perfect, and most have problems that can be easily fixed. However, serious problems, such as mold, water damage, deterioration, termites, or structural issues, may be grounds to cancel the contract, get your deposit back, and start shopping for another home.

Has anything changed?

A day or two prior to closing, arrange to take a final walk-through the house. Have your real estate agent accompany you. Make sure that the house is in the condition you expected and as it was when it was inspected.

If your agent, the inspector, or you have photographs of the home, bring them with you. During the walk-through, check for recent damage or whether items that were to be included in the sale have been removed. If you detect any problems, have your agent address them with the seller prior to closing.

What is the closing?

The big day is here! The last legal formality is the closing or transferring of title, which usually takes place at the title company office or at one of the lawyers' offices. Closings normally take less than an hour; in fact, they often run half that time. In most case, all documents have been prepared and are awaiting your signature. Frequently, the seller will have signed the papers in advance, but he or she may also come to the closing.

At the closing, the attorney or the title company officer will explain what all of the documents mean and their terms. He or she will also review the closing statement, which is a balance sheet that lists all the expenses involved in the transaction. The closing statement will give the exact figure you must pay to take title.

Occasionally, problems arise at closings that must be solved before title can be transferred. Sometimes, issues that were supposed to be resolved have not been concluded, so financial adjustments will be made. Frequently, sufficient money is set aside to fix the problem and held in trust pending resolutions. When this occurs, short agreements may be drafted and closing statements rewritten to reflect what occurred.

When you sign the mortgage and closing documents and provide the seller, or his or her agent, with a certified check, you will receive the keys to your new home. Within the next few days, the attorneys or title company officers will record the legal documents, and copies will be sent to you.

My Rx

Although easily obtainable mortgages played a dominant role in creating the present financial mess, an equally serious underlying problem helped it along: people took on obligations that were beyond their means. Because getting credit was so easy, they abandoned logic and the common-sense lessons they had been taught. They bought the homes they wanted, rather than buying only what they needed. And now, they're paying the price.

Get back to basics. Buy a home that you can afford and that will still leave you with money to save, invest, and let you enjoy your life. Scale down your present wants and build for tomorrow.

CHAPTER 14
WASTING MONEY ON
A LIFETIME OF CARS

THE AILMENT

After our homes, cars are the costliest items that most of us buy. In the course of our lives, we will buy as many as 10 to 15 cars, so how we buy and finance our cars can make a huge difference in our financial health.

Years ago, most families had one car, which they kept until it died of old age. Today, families tend to have more than one car and will buy a new one every four or five years. Additionally, many people trade up more frequently.

The problem is that cars are both expensive and awful investments—in fact, they're not really investments. They are "de-investments," which is my term for assets that are guaranteed to decline in value. When you invest, you hope that the value of your investment will increase, but, when you buy a car, you know that its value will steadily drop. Because the main purpose of a car is to provide transportation, to get you from point A to point B, it may be time to rethink how you purchase cars.

Although the car manufacturers won't like it, I'm going to make a bold, but true, statement: unless you're wealthy, never buy a new car. It will damage your financial health.

DIAGNOSIS

Buying a new car is a poor use of money and guarantees buyers an immediate loss of wealth. A new auto is more expensive than a used car, as are its monthly payments and the cost of insurance. New cars immediately depreciate at an accelerated rate, so if you have to sell soon after you bought it, you're going to take a bath.

Let's say that you just bought an auto for $22,000. The salesman congratulated you for making such a great deal, and as you drive home, you feel like a million bucks. Actually, you should be crying, because you lost $4,400 the moment you left the lot. New cars lose about 20 percent of their value as soon as you take ownership. Then they depreciate anywhere from 6 to 13 percent annually. In the first year, you could lose $5,720 to $7,260. Ouch! The money you lost could have been saved or invested in assets that usually appreciate through time. If you buy 10 cars during your life at an average cost of $25,000 each, you will lose $65,000 to $82,000 in first-year depreciation alone. Buying a used vehicle costs far less and makes much more financial sense.

VITAL SIGNS

Being financially healthy means accumulating wealth, and we accumulate wealth by saving and investing. Let's take a look at how much we really lose during a lifetime of buying new cars.

Lets assume that we buy 10 new cars during our lifetime, one every five years between ages 20 and 70. Let's also say that the first-year depreciation is $6,500 on each car. Had we invested that $6,500 and received an annual 5 percent return, at age 75 we would have accumulated $437,535, which isn't chump change—in fact, it could be a nice retirement fund.

When you buy a new car, you also become exposed to a hidden danger that most people never consider, but that can cost them a lot. Let me explain. When most Americans buy new cars, they put down as little money as they can and finance the rest. Usually, they finance 90 to 100 percent. So if you buy a car for $30,000, put down $3,000, and finance the rest, you would be obligated to pay $27,000 plus interest during the term of your loan.

If, a month or two later, you were in an accident and totaled the car, your insurance would only pay you $23,000, which would be the reasonable value of the car at that time. Because you owed slightly less than $27,000 on your loan, you would be out nearly $4,000 plus the initial $3,000 you put down, and you would not have the car.

Treatment

Buy a two- or three-year-old vehicle that has just come off a lease. Through the years, the quality and reliability of cars have improved dramatically. Today's cars are built well and can be expected to run for at least 150,000 to 200,000 miles if they're properly maintained.

Many used cars, especially those less than four years old, have low mileage and look new. If you have them checked out mechanically, you won't have to worry about buying someone else's problem, and you can expect years of safe, dependable service.

If you buy a used car, the original owner has absorbed the early depreciation. Instead of paying $25,000, you may pay $17,000, which is 32 percent less than the original owner paid. You also have to finance much less, so your monthly payments, insurance, and fees will be lower. If you decide to sell the car, you'll get more of your money back, because your car will have held more of its value. During the course of your car-buying life, buying late-model used cars can save you lots of money.

Auto liquidators

When cars are returned to banks or finance companies at the end of leases, the lenders don't want the cars. They want to sell them as quickly as possible to get their money back, so they work with dealers that specialize in selling off-lease vehicles for lenders.

These dealers are called lender liquidation dealers or liquidators. Every month, liquidators receive a large numbers of recently returned cars. The liquidator I've bought cars from gets 1,500 cars a month. It takes the best 250, puts them in its showrooms, and sells them to walk-ins. Then, it wholesales the rest at auto auctions. Because lenders are eager to sell, their liquidators frequently sell returned cars below book value.

Liquidators work with a number of banks and leasing companies and are paid a commission or a percentage of the sales price of the vehicles they sell. The balance of the sale proceeds they receive are turned over to the lenders.

My local liquidator's showroom is filled with 150 to 200 cars, so there is always a good selection from which to choose. They look new, have low mileage (most have between 10,000 and 30,000 miles), have been cleaned up, and are certified as mechanically sound by the liquidator. Most cars are priced at 3 to 5 percent below book value. You can buy an extended warranty, finance your purchase through the liquidator, or lease or purchase it outright.

I've purchased six new-looking, dependable cars from a local liquidator. I bought each for less than book value and have always been pleased. Buying from a liquidator involves little or no haggling, because the cars are so well priced to begin with. Check the Internet or your local phone book to find liquidators.

Before you buy a car from a liquidator, get the Vehicle Identification Number (VIN) and check its history. A number of online services provide reports on cars' histories.

When you buy from a liquidator, the portion remaining on the vehicle's new-car warranty comes with your purchase. For example, if you buy a car that has a 50,000-mile or five-year warranty that has been driven only 29,500 miles in two years, the new-car warranty will protect you for 20,500 miles or three years, whichever comes first. And if you wish, you can purchase an extended warranty from the liquidator.

The American Automobile Association (AAA) has a free program under which its members can get special prices on new and used cars. Under the program, members tell AAA which cars they want, and AAA refers them to dealers that are participating in the program. The dealers have designated personnel who then work with the member.

Financing auto purchases

When you buy a new or late-model car, you can pay for it in a number of ways. If you have the money, you can pay cash; however, most people need to finance their purchases. Unfortunately, many buyers don't think much about financing decisions, which can be just as important as deciding what car to buy and how much to pay.

Never take a loan that runs for more than four years. Auto loans are like mortgages: the bulk of your payment initially goes to pay interest and then gradually decreases during the term of the loan. In the early years, you pay lots of interest, but not much principal. So if you try to sell the car in the first few years, you may not be able to get rid of it without writing a check, because you owe more on your loan than your car is worth. You may even have to use all or most of the proceeds to pay off your loan. When an auto loan runs for more than four years, you probably will be paying too much for the car, once you factor in all the interest and costs. Although longer-term loans have smaller monthly payments, bite the bullet so you can build more equity in your car more quickly.

Car salespeople will ask you what you can afford to pay each month, because they can structure any loan to meet your needs. You can end up with a long-term loan that has smaller monthly payments, but your total outlay will be far more in the long run. If you can't afford the payment on a four-year loan, don't buy the car. Make a down payment of at least 20 percent to maintain some equity and not owe more on the car than it's worth.

Zero- or low-interest financing

As I've stated, I feel strongly that people should never buy new cars, because they cost too much money. However, I'm realistic and know that people will buy new cars for a variety of personal reasons. If you must buy a new vehicle, try to finance it with a zero- or low-interest loan.

Dealers offer zero- and low-interest loans when the economy is slow and car sales are down. Even if you have the cash to buy the car outright, it makes good financial sense to take advantage of these dealer incentives, because zero-interest loans give you free money, which you can't beat! Keep your cash in the bank and earn interest on it or invest it.

Bank financing

Most banks will arrange a car loan for you, and frequently give you better terms than dealer financing on both new and used car purchases. The interest rate they charge will be based on your credit rating. Before you shop for a car, investigate car loans. Check with a few banks and lenders. Find out the going rates and terms so you will know how much you can afford to spend for your car. Interest rates make a difference. If you borrow $20,000 for five years at 4 percent, you will pay a total of $2,099.83 in interest, but at 8 percent, you will pay a total of $4,331.67—a difference of $2,231.84.

Auto clubs

Loans can be obtained through auto clubs and associations, such as AAA. The financing they provide usually comes from banks and other lenders. The auto clubs usually receive a small percentage of the loans they place, so their rates can be higher than banks and direct lenders.

Dealer financing

All dealers have arrangements with lending institutions to provide auto loans. Although dealer-arranged loans are convenient, they usually come at a higher cost. Car dealers frequently get a cut of the loans they place, so you can usually do better with a bank.

Dealers may also pad the interest rates they quote you to increase their profits on car sales. Often, they won't tell you what interest rate you will be charged, but will only give you the dollar amount of your monthly payment. Dealers will try to entice you to take long-term loans, for as many as seven years, to lower the amount of your monthly payments and help get you into the car.

When some dealers explain financing and terms to you, they will overwhelm you with a flurry of words and numbers. Make sure that you understand everything they tell you, especially the loan's terms. If all the terms are not clear, question them until you fully understand. If, after you ask a number of questions, you still don't understand, get up and walk away.

Home equity loans

Although I believe in building equity in our homes and not tapping into it for current needs, it may make sense to borrow on a home equity loan to buy a car. The interest rate on a home equity loan may be lower than those for traditional auto loans, and they may allow you to make more flexible or extended payments. Most importantly, the interest on home equity loans is tax deductible in most cases.

Top new-car-buying rules

Most of us would rather go to the dentist than endure the torture of buying a car. Dealing with relentless, high-pressure salespeople is anything but fun, plus it can be very expensive. When you deal with car salespeople, you constantly feel manipulated and know deep down that you'll probably end up on the wrong end of the stick.

Everyone knows that car dealers have bags of tricks up their sleeves to maximize their profits, but few know how to counter them. This can cause most people to dread going to car dealerships because they hate feeling that they will be overwhelmed, overmatched, and coerced into paying far more than they should.

Car buying is an unfair experience. Two people can walk into the same car dealership, buy identical cars, and pay different prices for them—and the difference can amount to thousands of dollars. Unfortunately, women and the elderly are most vulnerable to auto dealers' tricks. Car salespeople know how to prey on them. Understanding the car-buying process and preparing well can help level the playing field and ensure that you strike a better deal.

The most important rule in buying a car is to be prepared *before* you walk into your friendly neighborhood car dealership. Do some homework, plan your attack, and give yourself enough time to make the best deal.

Preparing to buy

Here's some advice that will help you prepare for buying a car:

1. Identify your needs. Know beforehand what you're looking for as specifically as you can. Ask yourself questions such as:

   ☑ Do I need automatic or manual transmission?

   ☑ Do I need large cargo carrying capacity?

   ☑ Do I want a sedan or SUV?

   ☑ What gas mileage is acceptable?

   ☑ Which safety features and options are important to me?

2. Get a copy of your credit report and FICO score at *www.annualcreditreport.com*. Download your credit report and print out a copy. Your credit score will determine the interest rate you will have to pay on an auto loan. Visit your bank to see what terms it will give you on a car loan. Also research the terms car dealers, auto clubs, and other lenders are offering. Assume you will

be financing a maximum 80 percent of the purchase price and find out the terms of 48-month loans.

A family's monthly car payments should not exceed 20 percent of its monthly take-home pay. At *www.edmunds.com* you can find financial calculators to help you estimate your monthly payment. That payment will be based on the purchase price, down payment, interest rate, and length of loan. Print or write out the figures and bring them with you when you shop for a car.

3.   Don't forget to consider all ownership costs. Inquire into the cost of insurance for each vehicle you are considering, because those costs can vary greatly. Insurance costs are linked to car safety, which is information you should know and use as bargaining points with car salespersons.

Also consider depreciation; a car that may be less expensive than another car could depreciate at a faster rate, which would make it more expensive in the long run. Factor in each car's gas mileage, service program, warranty, and repair costs when determining the car's long-term cost.

4.   Before you buy a new car, find out your present car's fair market value at *www.kbb.com*, *www.edmunds.com*, or *www.nadaguides.com*. Then try to sell it privately, because you can usually get a better price than if you trade it in. Here's what to do:

☑   Place an ad on Craigslist (*www.craigslist.org*), or in your local newspaper or advertiser.

☑   Accept payment only in cash or by certified check, or you could get burned.

☑ Immediately after the sale, file any required papers with the state, so if the car is then involved in an accident, you won't be legally liable.

5. If you decide to trade in your car, determine your car's fair market value. Expect to be lowballed. New-car dealers will try to give you as little as possible for your car, because they plan to resell it, and the less they pay, the more they make. They will find problems with parts that you never knew existed.

Although dealers won't offer you the full value for your car, the fact that you know your car's actual value can help you negotiate a better price. However, don't expect to get as much as you would by selling your car on your own.

Negotiate the price of the new car first, and then discuss your trade-in. Because you're there to buy a new car, focus on it and don't let the salesperson divert you by starting negotiations on your trade-in.

6. The Internet is loaded with lots of great information on buying cars. Dealers have created Internet sites that allow car buyers to shop online. If you go online, you can check dealers' inventories, search the options available, and find out how much cars cost. Also look into dealer incentives such as rebates and zero-percent financing. Once you've narrowed down the vehicles you're interested in, go to a dealer for a test drive and negotiate a deal.

7. Learn how much the dealer has paid for the car before you negotiate. Forget about the sticker price or Manufacturer's Suggested Retail Price (MSRP); it's primarily for show. What really counts is how much the dealer has invested in the car.

To find the dealer's cost, go to *www.edmunds.com* and download dealer invoice prices. In most cases, a dealer will accept $500 to $1,000 more than its invoice price. On popular models, you may have to pay closer to the sticker price. Because these models are in demand, dealers don't have to discount them.

Find out all the additional costs you will have to pay, including taxes, registration, and destination charges. Make sure that you need or want what the dealer is trying to sell you. If the dealer claims that something you don't want comes with the car, insist that the dealer take it off. Don't pay for delivery, handling, floor charges, or any other unnecessary charges the dealer tries to bill you for.

8. One of the oldest tricks in the book and one of the first questions a salesperson will ask is how much you can afford to pay each month. Even though you already determined that before you went to the dealer, don't answer. If you do, it will give the salesperson the upper hand, because he or she can structure a loan to both fit within your figure and get his or her price for the car. Always negotiate the sales price on the vehicle itself—never on the monthly payment amount!

9. When you find the perfect car, don't gush or show your excitement. Play it cool, because when salespeople sense that you're head over heels about a car, they move in for the kill, and it becomes much tougher to negotiate a great deal. Take time to look at the deal more objectively. Ask yourself:

☑ Is it the right car for me?

☑ Does it have everything I want or is it loaded with too much?

☑ Am I prepared to take on the expenditures necessary to buy this car?

10. Dealers count on buyers acting impulsively. They know that people fall in love with cars and will go for terrible deals. Once you give them a glimmer of hope, they will push you to close the deal.

If you think the salesperson has offered you the best deal and you are ready to buy, let time work for you. Tell him or her that if you buy the car, you will buy it from him or her, but you need a little time to digest all of the information you received.

The salesperson will do everything possible to convince you to buy now (especially if it's the end of the month), including saying that the deal is only good for that day. Believe me, if you come back three days later, he or she will make the same deal.

After you leave the showroom, some salespeople will phone you relentlessly to convince you to close the deal. Think twice before you give them your phone number.

Take time to reflect on the deal, to make sure it's the car you want and that you can afford it. Be certain that you understand your total costs and that you got the best financing available. When you feel comfortable with your decision, go in and buy the car.

11. After you agree on a deal with the salesperson, he or she will escort you to the business manager's office. As he or she completes the paperwork, he or she will try to squeeze more money out of you by attempting to sell you dealer add-ons such as rust-prevention undercoating, sealants, auto-theft-recovery systems, insurance, and extended warranties.

These extras are expensive and their costs can mount up. Usually, they are unnecessary; say no thanks and complete the deal. The manager or salesperson may press you, but stand firm, because they usually won't risk losing the deal.

Auto Leasing

Leasing allows many people to buy cars they otherwise couldn't afford. By leasing a car, they actually rent the right to use it for a period of time, such as 36 months, 48 months, and so on.

Monthly lease payments consist of two components: depreciation and interest. Because those who lease never own the car, they pay only for the portion of the car's value during the lease period.

Leasing has some short-term advantages over buying, such as:

☑ The amount you have to initially put down to lease a car is usually less than what you put down if you bought it.

☑ The monthly payments are lower than if you bought the same car and financed it with an auto loan.

☑ Leasing expensive luxury cars for business can provide tax advantages. When you lease a car, the interest is rolled into the monthly payment, making it tax deductible. In contrast, interest paid on car loans is not tax deductible.

☑ After the lease expires, the car can be turned in and you can lease a new car, which works excellently for those who want to have a new car every few years.

Financially, the disadvantages of leasing far outweigh the advantages.

☑ You never build equity in your vehicle, because you never actually own it. You only have the right to use it.

☑ You always have car payments. If you buy a car and the loan term expires, your payments stop. Because cars are now manufactured to run dependably for as much as 200,000 miles, you can own a car for a long time after you have stopped making payments.

☑ If you exceed the maximum allowed mileage on a lease, you have to pay an overage charge when the lease is up. If you put on excess miles, you can be hit for a hefty payment.

☑ It's hard to terminate a lease early. Penalties are involved and all the charges can be costly.

☑ When your lease is up, you can be charged for wear and tear, which can be significant.

☑ If you decide to buy the car when the lease is up, it can be very expensive. You might have to get a loan to finance your purchase.

☑ Leasing contracts are very confusing. Often, you have no idea how much you're actually paying to lease the car.

☑ In the long run, leasing is more expensive then buying a car.

My Rx

I know how exciting it can be to buy a great-looking new car. It can impress your friends and neighbors, tell the world you've arrived, and make you feel like a million bucks. However, after a while, your excitement and your car's shiny new finish will fade, but your car payments won't; their expense will stay with you for years.

Be patient. Save yourself money across the board—on your down payment, monthly payments, insurance, and on the car's resale value—by buying a reliable two- or three-year-old car. You can find loads of them that look and run as if they're brand new. Then invest the money you saved to build your wealth.

CHAPTER 15
IMPROPER AND OVERLY EXPENSIVE INSURANCE COVERAGE

THE AILMENT

Insurance costs us a bundle. It's one of the largest items in most of our budgets, and its costs continue to spiral up. In the United States, most families spend between 10 and 15 percent of their annual income on insurance, some of which could be saved.

To live in our crowded, complex, and litigious society, we need insurance. Lawsuits are a constant threat, because people will sue for virtually any reason, and juries have returned huge judgments that many of us could never afford to pay.

At the same time, the costs of healthcare, long-term care, and auto repair have skyrocketed and are continuing to soar to new heights. Life has become so expensive that most people can't save and build wealth, so they buy life insurance policies in order to provide for their families after they're gone.

DIAGNOSIS

As with many personal finance problems, the culprit is ignorance. Many people don't understand insurance and most misunderstand its purpose. They believe that it should reimburse them, dollar-for-dollar, for the losses they incur. At one time, that formula may have applied, but now it no longer makes financial sense—it's become far too expensive.

The purpose of insurance today is to protect you from catastrophic loss, from losing everything for which you worked: if your home burns down and you don't have fire insurance, it could wipe you out. The same holds true for health and auto insurance. We buy health and auto policies so that we won't have to pay gigantic claims and bills.

When we buy insurance, we transfer the risk of catastrophic losses to insurance companies that then assume those risks. We pay insurance companies premiums to protect us from risks that are too expensive for us to take.

VITAL SIGNS

We hope that we never need insurance, but most of us can't do without it. We need to insure our cars, our health, our lives, our homes, and our incomes. Many people don't have disability insurance that insures their incomes, though it's far more likely that they will become disabled than die during their working years. Long-term healthcare insurance can also be vital. Some people need flood insurance, earthquake insurance, malpractice insurance, errors and omissions insurance, and much more.

Whatever type of insurance is bought, it seems that people don't shop around. They simply turn to someone they know in the business or someone who has been recommended to them. When people buy their first homes, their mortgage lenders require them to get fire and title insurance, which their real estate agents and title searchers usually arrange. Through the years, they tend to keep dealing with the same insurance agent, especially if they get decent service. Some people lean on their brokers and agents for advice. However, these people are salespersons who work on commission and may be more motivated by how much they can make than in providing the best, most cost-effective protection for their clients.

Because insurance is of such importance, find a specialist who can give you expert advice on your insurance needs. Look for an agent whom you trust, one who has a good reputation and comes highly recommended. Then meet with him or her and see if you feel comfortable. If so, discuss your existing coverage and your needs.

TREATMENT

The purpose of insurance is not to pay you dollar-for-dollar for your losses. Instead, insurance exists to protect you from catastrophic losses. If you're willing to take on more of the risk, the cost of insurance will be less. Higher deductible amounts will cut the amount of your premiums. The premium on a policy with a $1,000 deductible will be less than a policy with a $250 or $500 deductible. Although no one wants to pay a $1,000 deductible, it won't wipe you out. However, it will reduce the amount of your premiums. Higher copayments will also reduce your health insurance premiums. In most cases, small health-insurance deductibles and copayments are not cost effective.

Life insurance

Term insurance is pure insurance. You purchase a specific amount of insurance for a specific term. All you pay for is to insure the life of the insured. A term life insurance policy can run from one to 30 years, and it pays the face amount of the policy to the beneficiary. In level term policies, the premiums stay the same for the life of the policy.

Whole life insurance combines a death benefit with a savings component. You purchase it to insure you for your whole life, not just a specific term. The savings component helps the policy build cash value that can be borrowed against. Life insurance agents love to sell you whole life insurance policies because the premiums are higher and they get higher commissions.

Universal life insurance is whole life insurance, but you determine how much you want to contribute to the investment vehicle.

The insurance company chooses the investments and the returns go into an account that you can build or use to pay premiums.

Variable life insurance is also a form of whole life that allows policy owners to invest in a variety of separate accounts that are similar to mutual funds. The income from the investments builds up cash value. The term *variable* means that policy owners can invest in funds that vary in value.

With both whole life and term policies, you can lock in the same monthly payment during the life of the policy.

I like 20-year level term insurance policies. The annual premiums for term insurance policies are about a quarter of those of whole life insurance policies. Because whole life policies are so expensive, many people who buy these policies are underinsured. For example, Thomas pays $1,000 a year for a whole life policy that insures him for $100,000. However, for the same amount, Thomas could buy a term policy that insures him for $500,000.

As a savings or investment vehicle, whole life is preferable to term life. But for straight insurance, term life is cheaper, and you get more coverage for your money.

How much life insurance do you need?

The amount of insurance needed varies with each person's situation. If you're single and have enough assets to pay your debts and burial expenses, you may not need any life insurance. However, if you have a family, you probably want them to be able to live comfortably after you've gone. In addition, if your children are young or have disabilities or other problems, they will require more funds.

To determine how much your survivors will need, start by answering the following basic questions:

☑ How important is your income to your family? Can they live comfortably without your income or life insurance proceeds? Does your spouse have a well-paying job or other income sources that would let him or her live well without your income? If so, you will need less life insurance.

☑ Do you have large debt to pay? Many people want to have enough insurance to pay off their mortgage and all their existing debt when they die.

☑ Will funds be needed for your kids' education?

☑ How much money will your family need to live comfortably?

Let's look at the following family. Both the husband and wife are in their early 30s, and they have two young children. The husband earns $100,000 and the wife stays home with the kids. They have a $200,000 mortgage on their home.

I would advise this family to insure the husband's life for a minimum of $900,000. That amount would enable his wife to pay-off the mortgage and have another $200,000 to go into the kids' college fund. The remaining $500,000 balance could then be invested and produce a good income stream. A 20-year term policy would cost the family less than $1,000 a year, which I think is a great investment.

Auto insurance

Car insurance premiums can vary widely among insurance companies, and chances are you're paying more than necessary. If you spend a few hours shopping each year, you may be able to lower your costs substantially. However, most of us don't bother, and keep the same company for years.

Lower your auto insurance premiums by:

☑ Checking the Internet for quotes from all the companies offering auto insurance in your state. If you work with an insurance agent, a few weeks before it's time to renew your policy, ask him or her shop for better rates for you. I prefer to shop on my own, because insurance agents may have a conflict of interest and prefer to sell certain companies' policies.

☑ Contacting the company that insures your home for a discount for having multiple policies with it. Also look into insuring all your family's cars with the same company to cash in on multiple-car discounts.

☑ Maintaining a good driving record. Traffic violations and accidents make you a greater risk, so insurance companies will charge you more. If you're convicted of driving under the influence of alcohol, your insurance premiums will skyrocket for up to five years.

☑ Buying less expensive cars. The more expensive the car, the more it will cost to insure it.

☑ Dropping your collision coverage on older cars that are not worth much. At a certain point, many older vehicles are not worth fixing. Even if you have collision, it may be time for a change.

☑ Taking advantage of all discounts offered, such as those for having a good driving record, taking drivers training courses, and having vehicles with anti-theft devices and certain safety features. Ask what discounts are offered and see if you qualify for them.

☑ Joining an auto club, such as AAA, because you may be eligible for money-saving discounts. Your affiliation with professional organizations and groups may also make you eligible for discounts.

☑ Increasing your deductible. If you assume more of the risk, it can drastically lower your premium. Instead of a $500 deductible for collision, raise it to $1,000 or even $1,500.

Disability insurance

If you're out of work, disability insurance will replace your income. These policies are also called income replacement insurance. Most people don't have disability insurance, but they should consider it, because if they get hurt and their income ceases, disability insurance can help them pay their bills and avoid falling into debt. If you have a physically demanding job, it may be especially worthwhile for you.

Many companies offer disability insurance to their employees in lieu of a portion of their salaries. They also deduct the premiums from employees' pre-tax salary, which provides tax advantages for those employees.

Two types of disability policies are available: short-term disability (STD) policies and long-term disability (LTD) policies. With STD, you must to wait up to 14 days for your payments to kick in, and the maximum benefit period is usually two years. LTD policies require you to wait longer for your benefits to start—usually for several weeks or even months, depending on the policy. However, the benefits can last for years or even your lifetime.

Disability policies cannot be cancelled as long as you pay your premiums. Each year, you have the right to renew the policy, but your premiums can be increased provided they are also increased for all policy holders in your classification.

Health insurance

The biggest premiums that most families pay are for health insurance. Through the years, the cost of health insurance has consistently increased and outstripped the rate of inflation, and health insurance premiums are expected to continue to increase.

Unfortunately, many people have no health insurance or they're underinsured.

If you work for a company, you probably won't have much say in the type of health insurance you can have. In most cases, employers shop around, decide how much they're willing to spend, and then get a group plan to cover all their employees. Employees have some options regarding deductibles and copayments that can lower their payment amounts.

If you are self-employed, retired, or unemployed, you must do your homework and find the right policy for you. If you have just started a new business or are unemployed, it's important to get a cost-effective policy. Because health insurance is usually the lion's share of your insurance budget, it is important to keep the cost down.

Fee-for-service plans

Under these plans, you can choose your doctor or hospital. Typically, your insurance company pays 80 percent and you pay 20 percent of all bills, but a cap or ceiling amount is placed on your out-of-pocket cost. When you reach that cap, the insurance company pays 100 percent of your medical bills. Fee-for-service plans have annual deductibles for individuals and families that must be met before their benefits kick in. Usually they run from $250 to $500 annually. Some services might not be covered under fee-for-service plans, such as vaccinations or well care (preventative care including checkups and vaccinations).

Two basic types of fee-for-service plans exist: basic coverage and major medical. Basic coverage reimburses you for hospital care and includes x-rays and surgery. Major medical policies cover doctors' visits and all other services that basic excludes.

Health maintenance organizations (HMOs)

For a monthly premium, HMOs provide comprehensive family medical care. Because it's in their best interests that their members stay healthy, HMOs cover preventative healthcare such as vaccinations, checkups, mammograms, therapy, hospital stays, x-rays, and doctor visits. HMOs usually enroll local physicians to provide medical services and charge a small copayment for each doctor visit or hospital care.

HMO patients are limited to using physicians and facilities in the HMO network. With most HMOs, you select a primary physician, and that physician monitors your health and refers you to specialists in the network as needed. They also don't make you fill out all sorts of claim forms. HMOs offer the most cost-effective healthcare, but have limited flexibility regarding your provider choices.

Preferred provider organizations (PPOs)

A PPO is a more flexible HMO plan. It combines the features of HMO and fee-for-service plans. You pay a deductible and a small copayment for services. If you use the services of doctors and facilities in the network (the preferred providers), the majority of your bills is covered by your insurance company.

PPOs differ from HMOs because you can use doctors or hospitals out of the network. Your insurance company will pay for only a part of their charges, whereas an HMO will generally not pay for out of network services. With PPOs, you have a primary physician and limited number of doctors and hospitals that you can use. PPOs are more expensive than HMOs, but not as much as fee-for-service plans.

Long-term healthcare insurance

Because people are living longer, they have more time during which they may develop serious medical problems. Many can't take care of themselves and need assistance. Treatment in the average skilled nursing home costs between $3,000 and $7,500 a month, and home healthcare workers cost about $25 an hour. Because medical insurance or Medicare does not cover those expenses, long-term healthcare policies can be purchased to defray all or part of the costs.

Long-term care policies are expensive; many people can't afford them. The younger you are when you take out a long-term care policy, the lower your premium will be. If you wait, you may not qualify for a policy because of your health issues.

Long-term care policies usually cover:

☑ Nursing home care.

☑ Adult daycare.

☑ Assisted living services in facilities other than your home.

☑ Home care assistance for bathing, cleaning, eating, and dressing.

Long-term care policies can be confusing so make sure you understand the basics.

☑ Coverage. Different types of coverage can be purchased. They range from those that insure only home healthcare services to more comprehensive coverage that pays for nursing homes and assisted living facilities.

☑ Daily benefit. The daily benefit is the amount the insurance company will pay for each day that service is required. Choose a policy that will cover the entire estimated cost of care. If your expenses exceed the daily benefit amount, you will have to pay the difference.

☑ Inflation protection. Inflation protection adjusts the daily benefit amount for inflation. Hopefully, you won't need this policy for years, but when that time comes, the cost of healthcare will be more expensive. So inflation protection is a must!

☑ Waiting period. Also known as the elimination period, it is the number of days you have to wait before the policy begins covering expenses. Waiting periods can range from 0 to 100 and the premiums will vary accordingly. The longer the waiting period, the lower the premium.

☑ Benefit period. The maximum amount of time the policy will pay benefits. You can choose a two-year benefit period, or it can run for your lifetime. The average nursing home stay is 2 1/2 years, so a three- or four-year benefit period should be fine.

☑ Premium waiver. These allow you to stop paying premiums when you enter a nursing home.

The decision of whether or not to buy long-term care insurance can be particularly hard. Do you buy an expensive policy that you could be paying for years or do you risk incurring large expenses in the future? The answers to the following questions may help you decide.

☑ Do you have significant assets that could be depleted if you need long-term care? If you don't have a lot of money or if your income is low, you most likely can't justify paying the premium.

☑ Is there a history of Alzheimer's disease in your family? Nursing home patients suffering from Alzheimer's disease tend to stay in nursing homes much longer than patients with other heath issues.

☑ Can you afford the premium? Long-term care policy premiums can be as much as $4,000 to $5,000 a year. Think about whether your budget can handle such a large payment. Insurers can and have increased initial premiums drastically in the past. Decide if you can handle a big hike in premiums down the line. It would be a shame if you had to cancel a policy because of a premium increase after you paid years worth of premiums.

If you decide to purchase long-term care insurance, make sure you take your time, shop around, and ask many questions about each policy's features. Also check the financial health of the insurance company. You may not need the benefits for many years, so you want to be sure the insurance company is healthy enough to still be in business when it's your turn to tap benefits.

My Rx

Allow me to illustrate how important it is to have insurance, using an experience I had with a client.

Early in my career, I met John and Mary, a young couple who had two small children. John was struggling to make ends meet and said he could not afford to buy life insurance. A friend had tried to sell him a $300,000 whole-life policy that cost $2,400 a year. It was much more than he could afford, so he passed on it. I asked him if I could review the proposal.

A few days later, I presented John with a proposal for a 20-year level term-life policy with a $500,000 death benefit. The premium was less than $500 a year. Because it would give him a larger benefit at only 20 percent of the whole life insurance cost, John eagerly bought the policy.

Six months later, Mary called and told me that John died in an accident at work. I'll never forget the feeling I had knowing that I was able to provide John with low-cost insurance so that Mary and her children would not be in financial danger. I knew that life insurance was important, but that day I learned how crucial having the proper insurance really is.

Insurance, whether it's life, car, health, or any other necessary type, is vital. Without it you could lose much of your net worth, and, in the event a catastrophe occurred, you could fall deeply in debt. Lack of proper insurance coverage is like driving your car without a seatbelt; if an accident occurs, it could destroy your financial body.

CHAPTER 16
EXCEEDING
FDIC LIMITS

THE AILMENT

When the economy went into the recent downturn, many banks failed. Although the government propped up a number of large banks, a lot of smaller and mid-sized banks folded. When those banks went under, many people lost substantial amounts of money, because their deposits exceeded the Federal Deposit Insurance Corporation's (FDIC) insurance limits.

There is no reason why anyone should lose money because their bank deposits exceed the FDIC insurance limits. The FDIC now insures basic savings accounts for $250,000 per individual account per bank. It also insures other accounts that are owned by the same depositor for up to $250,000, based on the title of those accounts, such as single accounts, joint accounts, certain retirement accounts, trust accounts, and corporation, partnership, and unincorporated association accounts.

DIAGNOSIS

Because the U.S. banking system had been so stable for so long, many depositors never imagined that their banks would fail. When they placed their funds in banks, they believed that they were putting their money in the safest place. In fact, many willingly took smaller returns for the safety they felt they were receiving from banks.

Many depositors put money in bank accounts without ever thinking that their deposits might exceed the FDIC limits. In many cases, they never knew what those limits were and how they could protect their funds. Once again, ignorance was the culprit. People blindly put their money in banks without ever actually knowing how much protection their funds would receive.

When IndyMac Bank failed in July 2008, depositors lost more than $1 billion because their accounts exceeded the FDIC insurance limits. Some 10,000 accounts were over the FDIC limits. When Nevada-based Silver State Bank, which was much smaller, went under, it had more than $20 million in uninsured funds.

According to industry scuttlebutt, before the FDIC's 2008 increase in insurance limits, as much as 40 percent of bank deposits were estimated to be uninsured. Although much of those uninsured funds were held by institutions and small businesses, many individual accounts were over the insurance limit as well.

The problem persists. In May 2009, the FDIC's list of troubled banks soared to 305, a 21 percent increase from the fourth quarter of 2008. FDIC chairwoman Sheila Bair warned that many banks will fail before the financial crisis is over. More than 50 banks failed during the first six months of 2009.

VITAL SIGNS

The FDIC was created in 1933 to insure funds deposited in U.S. banks. Prior to that time, money in U.S. banks was not insured. So when thousands of banks failed during the Great Depression of the late 1920s and early 1930s, millions of people lost their life savings. To prevent such wide-scale catastrophes from happening again, the FDIC was founded.

FDIC insurance took the risk out of depositing money in banks. Since it's founding, no depositor has ever lost any FDIC-insured funds. By insuring bank deposits, the FDIC prevents runs on banks, which were common before 1933. By preventing runs, the FDIC made the U.S. banking system more stable.

Since 1980, the FDIC has insured accounts for up to $100,000. In October 2008, the insurance limits were temporarily raised to $250,000 per account. That increase is scheduled to end on December 31, 2013, and the old $100,000 per-account limit is to return. However, the $250,000 ceiling will remain on IRAs and other retirement accounts.

FDIC insurance covers bank accounts held in a banking institution. Deposits in separate branches of that banking institution are not separately insured. Therefore, if you have $100,000 deposited at each of three separate branches of X Bank, only $250,000 of your deposits will be covered by the FDIC.

All insured institutions that provide FDIC insurance must display an official FDIC sign at each teller window or teller station. To check on whether your bank has FDIC coverage use Bank Find at *www2.fdic.gov/idasp/main_bankfind.asp* or call 1-877-ASK-FDIC. You can then use the FDIC online calculator—EDIE the Estimator—at *www.fdic.gov/edie/index.html* to see if your accounts are insured.

When depositors place funds with an FDIC-covered bank, coverage is automatic. Depositors do not have to apply for FDIC insurance or even request it. FDIC insurance protects money in deposit accounts, including checking and savings accounts, joint accounts, business accounts, money market deposit accounts, and Certificates of Deposit (CDs).

The FDIC provides separate coverage for deposits held in different types of accounts. Each of the accounts listed in the chart on page 178 can be in the same institution and each will be insured up to $250,000. The chart also assumes that all FDIC requirements are met (for details on the requirements, go to *www.fdic.gov/deposit/deposits*).

FDIC Deposit Insurance Coverage Limits
(Through December 31, 2013)

Single accounts (owned by one person)	$250,000 per owner
Joint accounts (two or more persons)	$250,000 per co-owner
IRAs and certain retirement accounts	$250,000 per owner
Revocable trust accounts	$250,000 per owner per beneficiary up to five beneficiaries (More coverage is available with six or more beneficiaries subject to specific limitations and requirements)
Corporation, partnership, and unincorporated association accounts	$250,000 per corporation, partnership, or unincorporated association
Irrevocable trust accounts	$250,000 for the non-contingent, ascertainable interest of each beneficiary
Employee benefit plan accounts	$250,000 for the non-contingent, ascertainable interest of each plan participant
Government accounts	$250,000 per official custodian

For example, Sara will be fully insured if she has the following amounts in one bank:

☑ $250,000 in a bank account in her name.

☑ $500,000 in a joint account with her husband, Marty. Each joint account owner can be insured up to $250,000.

☑ $250,000 in an IRA.

☑ $250,000 in each payable-on-death account (naming multiple survivors).

☑ $250,000 in her business partnership account.

So Sara can have more than $1 million in one bank and all her money will be fully insured. Her spouse, Marty, can also have $250,000 in an account in his name, an IRA in his name, his business account, and a payable-on-death account in the same bank, and it will be fully insured.

The FDIC's Website (*www.fdic.gov*) is packed with lots of easy-to-understand information. For questions about FDIC coverage, call toll-free 1-877-ASK-FDIC or speak with a representative at your bank.

Items not insured

The FDIC does not insure a number of items, even if they were purchased from an FDIC insured institution. They include:

☑ Stocks.

☑ Bonds.

☑ Mutual funds.

☑ Money funds.

☑ Annuities.

☑ Insurance (including life, auto, and homeowners).

☑ U.S. government–backed investments, such as U.S. Treasury securities.

☑ Contents of safe deposit boxes.

☑ Losses due to theft or fraud at the institution.

TREATMENT

Evaluate the health of your bank. Bauer Financial, Inc. and BankRate.com use star rating systems. They can be found at *www.bauerfinancial.com* and *www.bankrate.com/rates/safe-sound/bank-ratings-search.aspx?t=cb*, respectively. If you feel your bank's condition is weak, move your money to another institution.

Understand the FDIC insurance limits. Because the FDIC provides separate coverage for funds held in different types of accounts, learn what types of accounts you can put your money in and be fully protected.

Don't deposit sums that are not fully insured. If you want to deposit more than the FDIC limits, open different accounts or open accounts in other institutions. In these uncertain economic times, many banks are in a shaky financial condition, and some of them will fail, so be sure your money is fully protected!

Even though you can open a number of insured accounts, don't put all your money in one bank. If a systemic bank failure occurs and big banks go under, you don't want to have all your money tied up in one institution because you may not be able to get it quickly. Furthermore, if such a disaster should occur, no one knows exactly what the consequences will be, so it's best to play it safe.

My Rx

It's easy to make sure that all your money in the bank is insured. Your risk is easy to avoid. You don't have to go to lawyers, accountants, financial advisors, or jump through endless hoops. All you have to do is sit down with a banker and open different types of insured accounts. If, at any one bank, FDIC insurance won't cover all that you want to deposit, open accounts at another bank.

I expect the $250,000 FDIC limit to be made permanent, because returning it to $100,000 could hurt the banking industry, which is still running a fever. It's hard to reduce the amount of insurance after people deposited funds in reliance of the fact that they would be insured up to $250,000 per account.

CHAPTER 17
FAILING TO PLAN
FOR COLLEGE EARLY

THE AILMENT

Higher education costs a fortune. During the last 30 years, the cost of higher education has soared; it's gone up more than the rate of inflation. However, during that time, the need for higher education has also increased.

Many families have not been able to pay for their kids' post–high school education. Some families didn't save and others started saving too late. Many miscalculated; they thought they were putting enough aside, but the cost of higher education shot up far more than they expected—so they came up short. Others had the college investment accounts they established decimated by the stock market crash of 2008.

When parents can't pay for their children's education, they often leave their kids a legacy of debt. If their children want to continue their schooling, they must take out student loans, a sizeable debt. By the time they graduate, they may owe a couple hundred thousand dollars, which can strangle them financially, affect their credit, and take them decades to repay.

For many parents, funding their children's higher education jeopardizes their retirement plans. If they did not save, or save enough, they had to refinance their mortgages, take home equity loans, or tap into their 401(k) plans, depleting their retirement nest eggs.

DIAGNOSIS

More than ever, it's essential to have a higher education. Globalization has created intense competition for jobs, and workers abroad with comparable skills receive far less compensation than those in the United States, which sends many jobs overseas. Many jobs have also become more specialized, so candidates need more training to even apply for them.

Higher education is now more expensive across the board, whether it's through college or vocational, specialty, and graduate schools. If you want to be a chef, a sculptor, or a dental hygienist, it now costs more. At the same time, record numbers of students are attending graduate school, which prolongs their education and increases their expenses and debt.

The recent credit crunch has made student loans harder to obtain, and the economic downturn has forced more kids to enroll in less expensive community and state schools, instead of the more expensive institutions they probably would have attended in better times.

VITAL SIGNS

You can save for your child's education in a number of ways. Some offer substantial tax benefits, whereas others simply enable you to build education funds.

The funding methods I will describe can be complex, and the laws that govern them may differ from state to state. Before you try to use them, consult with experts such as lawyers, accountants, or financial advisors. Discuss these methods in detail, discover their advantages and disadvantages, and decide which are best for you.

CollegeSure CD

The return on this FDIC-insured CD is tied to college costs. When you buy a CollegeSure CD, you're essentially prepaying a child's college costs, because, at maturity, the CD is guaranteed to be enough to pay a fixed percentage of the average college costs. That percentage varies according to the cost of the CD you buy. When it matures, the CollegeSure CDs' funds—principal and interest—may be used to pay expenses at any school.

The CollegeSure CD, which is offered by College Savings Bank of Princeton, N.J., can be purchased for terms of 1 to 22 years and bought in whole or partial units. The interest it earns is taxable, and a penalty for early withdrawal may be charged. If the child doesn't attend college, you will receive the entire principal and interest at maturity to use as you wish.

You can make the CollegeSure CD tax-free by buying one of the two 529 College Saving Plans that the College Savings Bank (*www.collegesavingsbank.com*) administers. The College Savings Bank handles both the Montana and Arizona Plans, but anyone from any state can purchase them.

Coverdell accounts

These accounts were originally called education IRAs, even though they had nothing to do with retirement savings. They are also called Education Savings Accounts (ESAs). Coverdell accounts are created to pay the beneficiary's education expenses. To receive tax benefits, they must be created when the beneficiary is younger than 18 years old.

The beneficiary, or his or her parents, may own a Coverdell account. A maximum of $2,000 per beneficiary per year may be contributed until the beneficiary turns 18 years old. However, if parents earn too much, the amount that they contribute may be reduced or eliminated. For married taxpayers filing jointly, the $2,000 contribution limit begins to be phased out when the modified adjusted gross income (MAGI) exceeds $190,000, and it is totally phased out when the MAGI reaches $220,000. For single taxpayers, the $2,000 contribution limit begins to be phased out when the MAGI exceeds $95,000, and is totally eliminated when the MAGI reaches $110,000.

Contributions must be made in cash and stock; bonds or other savings vehicles are not acceptable. If the beneficiary does not use the money by age 30, it will be taxed as ordinary income and a 10-percent penalty will be assessed. Although contributions are not deductible from federal or state income taxes, the earnings grow tax-free, and qualified distributions are exempt from federal income tax.

Coverdell accounts have an advantage over other educational savings plans, because their funds can be used for private schools from kindergarten through high school. Account funds can be used to pay for tuition and supplies—you can even buy a computer with Coverdell funds.

Custodial accounts

These accounts are similar to trusts, but do not involve all the red tape or expense. A custodial account is established in the minor's name, and the parent, grandparent, or other relative or designee is the custodian. The custodian's job is to manage the funds in the account and make sure they are invested properly. The laws governing a custodial account differ from state to state.

The person who establishes a custodial account has little control over it. The money they put into a custodial account is an irrevocable gift for the minor, but the income earned by the account may be taxable income for the establisher. When the minor comes of age, the custodial account terminates. The minor can withdraw money and use it how he or she wishes; it doesn't have to be used to pay for his or her education.

Custodial accounts can be risky if they're established for problem, troubled, or extremely immature children. When they suddenly come into a big chunk of change, they often can't handle it and may blow it all.

Custodial accounts are also known as UGMA and UTMA, which mean Uniform Gifts to Minors Accounts and Uniform Transfer to Minors Accounts, respectively. UTMAs are the successor to UGMAs and allow more types of assets to be placed in these accounts. UTMAs provide some tax benefits, but not as much as 529 plans, especially when large amounts of money are involved. For further information about taxes on custodial accounts, see *www.fairmark.com/college/kidtax/kiddietax.htm*.

529 Savings Plans

529 savings plans are state or educational institution plans that allow you to put significant amounts of money into a plan. These plans are tax deferred. If the money is used for college, it's tax-free. More importantly, when you establish a 529 Savings Plan, you retain ownership of the money and control the account. You also decide when and how the funds will be withdrawn and spent. Under a 529 Plan, if the beneficiary is a problem or doesn't want to go to college, you can change the beneficiary to another child or have the funds reverted to you.

Contributions to a 529 Plan are not deductible from your federal taxes, but as the money you invest grows, your profits are tax-deferred and the distributions you use to pay college costs are free from federal taxation. If the money is not used for college, you will have to pay taxes on the plan's profits and in most cases a 10-percent penalty. It's best to use a 529 Savings Plan for education for yourself or someone else in your family. Some states also provide tax benefits for 529 plans, such as tax deductions for your contributions or exempting certain income that you withdraw.

Many 529 plans offer age-based investment options. That means that the younger the child is the higher the percentage of the investments will go into mutual funds that are stock market–oriented. As the child becomes older, less is invested in the stock market and more in the bond market. Shortly before the child is ready for college, the plan has invested virtually everything in conservative investments.

Due to a quirk in the law, each state must have its own 529 Plan. In each state, a specific mutual fund company or investment manager administers the plan for that state. However, anyone from any state can invest in any state's 529 Plan; you are not restricted to only your state's plan. Shop around to find out which plan is best for you.

You can buy 529 Plans directly from plan managers or through financial advisors. Many plans have no sales charges if you buy them directly from the firms that manage them. Plans purchased through financial advisors usually have sales charges or other fees.

Prepaid tuition plans

Many states and educational institutions offer prepaid college tuition plans that enable families to purchase all or part of their children's education at today's costs. In state plans, families that reside in the state can either make lump sum or periodic payments to lock in tuition costs at a state college or university. The states guarantee that the amounts families pay will grow at or above the rate of increases in college costs.

Plans at individual colleges also lock in tuition costs, but their provisions vary on a number of points. For example, what happens if a student graduates early, transfers, or drops out? Some state plans refund balances, whereas others prorate them or charge penalties. Review the terms of individual college plans carefully before getting involved in one.

TREATMENT

Start building an education fund for your child as soon as he or she is born. Don't wait. Even if you can only contribute a small amount, get the ball rolling. If you save $50 a month from the time your child is born and average a 7-percent return, you will have almost $22,000 when your child turns 18. Saving four times as much, or $200 a month, will give you more than $87,000 when your child comes of age.

Before you establish your education fund, speak with your parents and in-laws. They may be familiar with such funds, give you good advice, or recommend experts who can give you invaluable advice. Your parents or in-laws may also wish to establish an education fund because it's great way for them to pass some of their assets to their grandchildren.

The younger your child, the more aggressively you should invest the moneys in your education fund. As your child gets closer to college age, the more conservative you should become. If you monitor your investments closely, you should have plenty of time to make whatever adjustments you need.

MY RX

I think 529 plans offer the best options for higher education investment plans because they give you the greatest amount of tax benefits and plan flexibility. With a 529, you own the plan, and can change the beneficiaries and take back your money.

Although the financial crises and its impact on state governments have made the safety of prepaid tuition plans questionable, I do not believe that states will not make good on their promises to pay for children's higher educations. However, who knows what the situation will be 18 years from now.

It's less expensive to start early and contribute to a college fund year by year than to borrow when your child goes to college. When you save and invest, your money grows and compounds. When you borrow to pay for an education, you pay interest and your debt increases. In the long run, it makes financial sense to build a fund, rather than to borrow.

CHAPTER 18
ESTATE PLANNING
SHORTFALLS

THE AILMENT

No one likes to come to grips with his or her mortality, or to plan for his or her death. But by avoiding estate planning, people can saddle their loved ones with the overwhelming task of sorting everything out. Lack of planning complicates survivors' lives. Not having wills or advance directives—the basic requirements for good estate planning—puts survivors through needless expense and aggravation.

DIAGNOSIS

If you die without a will, what you own may not go to those whom you want to receive it. If you leave no legally binding directions on how your property should be divided, the government steps in. Then it decides where your property will go—which may not be where you want.

If you die without a will, you will put your survivors through a lot of needless work and expense. If you leave no instructions on how you want your assets distributed, your survivors may:

☑ Be required to post bonds, go to court, and cut through miles of sticky red tap.

189

☑ End up spending more time with lawyers than with their families.

☑ Not know to whom to give particular items.

☑ Get into ugly battles with each other.

VITAL SIGNS

Many young people don't believe they need estate planning. They feel immortal and think they have plenty of time to get their estates in order. They may also believe that they don't own enough to begin planning. However, if young people have children, they definitely need estate planning.

Here's why. In wills, parents name guardians for their children, the people they want to step in should anything happen to them. If those parents die without leaving a will, the state will decide who should serve as their children's guardian. It could appoint grumpy Uncle Gus, who has the best qualifications on paper, but whom your kids dislike. If parents have children with special needs, writing a will that designates who will serve as their guardian is especially important.

Last wills and testaments

Estate planning starts with your "last will and testament." Your will is the written document in which you designate how you want your assets distributed. Although your will directs where your possessions will go, a number of assets are not controlled by your will. They include the proceeds from retirement plans such as IRA and 401(k) accounts, variable and fixed annuities, pension plans, life insurance, and most jointly titled accounts.

Because some assets are not subject to your will, problems can arise that estate planning can avoid. If your will calls for your children to split everything you own equally, but all of your money is in an IRA and your son is the beneficiary, the funds in your IRA will pass outside your will. All of your kids, including your son, will split everything else, but only your son will be entitled to all IRA funds.

Moneys in joint bank accounts with the right of survivorship also pass outside your will. In other words, if you have an account in which your daughter has the sole survivorship rights, she will receive those funds regardless of what is stated in your will.

Parents often think that they should make their kids joint owners of their property. Frequently, older parents do it for their own convenience. They think that it will help them to have one of their children handling their finances, writing their checks, and paying their bills. However, problems can arise if more than one child is involved.

Mary thought it would be convenient to make her daughter Alice the joint owner of her home and sizable brokerage account. When Mary died, her home and brokerage account automatically transferred to Alice alone even though Mary's will provided that her son, Bob, and Alice should each receive half of her estate. Because Mary had hardly any other assets, her son was effectively disinherited.

Although Alice was not required to give Bob any part of her inheritance, she gave him half because that was what her mother would have wanted. However, Alice had to pay gift taxes on the money she gave Bob. The amount of her gift tax payment was far more than the amount estate planning would have cost.

When you write a will, you designate who will serve as the executor. Your executor is the person who administers your estate and distributes its assets. It's not a great job. If you want to get back at someone you don't like, make him or her the executor of your will.

Executors must liquidate the estate's assets, file all necessary documents and tax returns, pay bills, resolve all liabilities, and deal with impatient beneficiaries. In the process, executors may have to work with professionals including lawyers, accountants, financial advisors, and real estate brokers.

So an executor has to have financial acumen. He or she must know how to have assets valued, liquidate investments, file taxes, and resolve claims. An executor may have to run or oversee a business, investments, and complex financial trusts. He or she must be able to work with experts such as estate accountants, attorneys, and insurance agents.

Many people make the mistake of making their favorite child or relative their executor. Although their favorite may have been dear to them, he or she may not have the experience or ability to be a good executor. Name the most competent person to be your executor, not the person closest to you.

Parents who have two children frequently want to make them both executors. Co-executors often bang heads, because they have different loyalties and objectives. Make your most competent child your executor and name the other child as the alternate or successor executor if the other cannot or does not wish to serve.

Before you designate an executor, ask that individual if he or she is willing to serve. Tell that person what being an executor entails and what you want him or her to do. If you chose one child over another, explain your reasoning to both to prevent any hurt feelings or resentment.

Executors are entitled to be paid a fee for their services. Usually, it's a percentage of the value of the estate. Executors can also be liable for their actions or omissions, such as violating laws, making mistakes, or not submitting necessary documents or doing so on time.

Lawyers have a saying: "in-laws are outlaws." It means that your children may understand the reasons for the provisions in your will, and even if they don't, they will probably go along. But their spouses may not. Your children's spouses may feel short- changed or overlooked or that they, their spouse, or their children were deprived of bequests they should have received.

Advance medical directives

Wills give directions that are to be carried out after you die, whereas advance medical directives give instructions that are to take effect during your life. Advance medical directives are written documents that are legally binding and tell your medical providers what to do if you are unable to make decisions about your medical treatment. They also specify which individuals can make decisions on your behalf. Different types of advance directives exist, including living wills, do-not-resuscitate orders, healthcare proxies, and durable powers of attorney.

Advance directives are essential because they leave no doubt as to your wishes. They tell your medical providers and your survivors how you wish to be treated. Executing advance medical directives is especially important because your providers or survivors may disagree with your wishes.

Advance medical directives are called by different names in different states. Their requirements may also vary from state to state. Check with your healthcare provider or local healthcare associations for the requirements in your state.

Living wills

This document specifies the type of medical treatment you want to receive if you are incapacitated. It usually states that if you suffer an incurable, irreversible disease or condition, and your attending physician determines that you are terminally ill, that all measures to prolong your life be stopped.

Living wills may direct that you not receive CPR (do-not-resuscitate orders), dialysis, assisted breathing, or donated organs or tissue. They may also spell out the type of care and treatment you want to receive, especially if you have a particular medical condition.

In many states, hospitals will keep you on life support unless they have a signed, written document that specifically directs them not to. I've seen families torn apart because one child wanted to remove a feeding tube while the other was violently opposed to doing so.

Speak with your doctor about signing a living will. Many can give you forms to fill out and sign in the presence of witnesses.

Healthcare proxy

A healthcare proxy is a person whom you authorize to make healthcare decisions for you if you are incapacitated and cannot make your wishes known. The person you appoint has the right to request or refuse medical treatment for you.

Durable powers of attorney

These legal documents authorize the person you designate to execute legal documents and take legal action for you. For example, if you're confined to a bed, you can execute a power of attorney that lets your son write checks and do your banking for you, sign documents to buy and sell property for you, pay your bills, and handle your accounts.

Springing durable powers of attorney, also known as springing financial powers of attorney, do not take effect until you are certified as being incapacitated. Then they spring to life. Your designee cannot act on your behalf until you are certified as disabled.

Estate Letter of Instructions

One of the major benefits of estate planning is that it can make life much easier for your survivors. If you have lived a full life, you probably have records, files, and important papers that your survivors will need. Unfortunately, many people's personal records and information are in disarray. To prevent this problem, I developed a letter of instructions that you can fill out to give your survivors. They will bless you for it! The Estate Letter of Instructions is not a legal document, has no binding effect, and does not replace your will or other legal documents. It's simply an organizational and informational tool, but an extremely important one.

The Estate Letter of Instructions has a section for listing the names of those who are to get your personal items, things that are too minor to specify in your will. However, they may have great value to your survivors, and the decision of who receives these items can create conflicts within families. The last thing you want is for your family to fight or fall apart after you're gone. Putting your wishes in writing will help you rest in peace.

ESTATE LETTER OF INSTRUCTIONS

Name: _____ Date: _____

Social Security Number: _____

FIRST THINGS TO DO

1. Call _____ Telephone No.: _____

2. Make funeral home arrangements (See Cemetery and Funeral section)

3. Request at least 10 copies of the death certificate (Usually supplied by the funeral home)

4. Call Lawyer:

Name: _____ Telephone No.: _____

5. Provide obituary information to the following newspapers:

_____

_____

6. Contact Social Security Office.

7. Find and process life insurance policies (See Life Insurance section)

8. Notify the following people and organizations:

_____

EXPECTED DEATH BENEFITS

Life Insurance

Name of agent: _____ Telephone No. _____

Company   Policy Number   Death Benefit Amount

_____

_____

_____

Veterans Administration

Address: _____

Employer or former employer

Address: _____

Other sources and amounts

_____

_____

CEMETERY AND FUNERAL

Cemetery Plot

Name and location: _____

Date purchased: _____

Deed number: _____

Location of deed: _____

Other information (e.g. perpetual care or other arrangements):

_____

Facts for Funeral Director

Full name: _____

Residence: _____

Marital status: _____ Name of partner: _____

Date of birth: _____ Birthplace: _____

Mother's maiden name and birthplace: _____

Father's name and birthplace: _____

Length of residence in state: _____

In the United States: _____

Military record: _____

Dates of military service: _____

BANK ACCOUNTS

Bank name and address: _____

Name(s) on account: _____

Account number: _____

Type of account (circle one): Checking   Savings   CD

Location of checkbook/passbook/certificate: _____

Bank name and address: _____

Name(s) on account: _____

Account number: _____

Type of account (circle one): Checking   Savings   CD

Location of checkbook/passbook/certificate_____

Bank name and address: _____

Name(s) on account: _____

Account number: _____

Type of account (circle one):   Checking   Savings   CD

Location of checkbook/passbook/certificate: _____

INVESTMENTS

Financial advisor name: _____

Financial advisor firm: _____

Telephone No.: _____

Circle type of account: Mutual Fund   Brokerage   Annuity   IRA

Account number: _____

Location of recent statement: _____

Circle type of account: Mutual Fund   Brokerage   Annuity   IRA

Account number: _____

Location of recent statement: _____

Circle type of account: Mutual Fund   Brokerage   Annuity   IRA

Account number: _____

Location of recent statement: _____

Circle type of account: Mutual Fund   Brokerage   Annuity   IRA

Account number: _____

Location of recent statement: _____

LOCATION OF PERSONAL PAPERS

Last will and testament: _____

Birth and baptismal certificates: _____

Marriage certificate: _____

Naturalization papers: _____

Other (Adoption, divorce, deeds): _____

_____

INCOME TAX RETURNS

Location: _____

Tax preparer:

Name: _____ Telephone No.: _____

Circle whether you pay estimated quarterly taxes: Yes   No

CREDIT CARDS

All credit cards in the name of the deceased should be canceled or converted to the survivor's name.

Company: _____ Telephone No.: _____

Address: _____

Name on card: _____

Location of card: _____

Company: _____ Telephone No.: _____

Address: _____

Name on card: _____

Location of card: _____

Company: _____ Telephone No.: _____

Address: _____

Name on card: _____

Location of card: _____

Company: _____ Telephone No.: _____

Address: _____

Name on card: _____

Location of card: _____

LOANS OUTSTANDING

Lender's name and address: _____

_____

Name on loan: _____ Loan No.: _____

Monthly payment: _____

Circle if life insurance is on loan: Yes   No

Lender's name and address: _____

_____

Name on loan: _____ Loan No.: _____

Monthly payment: _____

Circle if life insurance is on loan: Yes   No

DEBTS OWED ESTATE

Debtor: _____

Description: _____

Terms: _____

Location of Documents: _____

Comments on loan status/discharge: _____

_____

Debtor: _____

Description: _____

Terms: _____

Location of Documents: _____

Comments on loan status/discharge: _____

_____

REAL ESTATE

Primary residence

Debtor: _____

Description: _____

Terms: _____ Balance: _____

Location of documents: _____

Comments on loan status/discharge: _____

_____

Secondary residence

Debtor: _____

Description: _____

Terms:_____ Balance:_____

Location of documents: _____

Comments on loan status/discharge: _____

_____

AUTOMOBILES

Year, make, and model: _____

VIN number: _____ Color: _____

Title in name of: _____

Location of papers: _____

Year, make, and model: _____

VIN number: _____ Color: _____

Title in name of: _____

Location of papers: _____

MEDICAL

Doctor's name:_____ Telephone No.: _____

Doctor's name:_____ Telephone No.: _____

Doctor's name:_____ Telephone No.: _____

PERSONAL PROPERTY DESIGNATION

Recipient	Item	Location

TREATMENT

Build a strong team filled with top professionals. Work with a lawyer, accountant, financial advisor, and insurance advisor. Start when you're young and building wealth, rather than waiting until you are older. Working with experts is a great investment.

As soon as you acquire any meaningful assets, write a will and make plans for the distribution of your property. Begin estate planning. Name the most competent person to be your executor and appoint guardians for your minor children.

Execute advance medical directives so that you get the type of medical treatment you want at the end of your life. Discuss your living will with your physician and then complete all necessary documents.

Make sure that you have enough life insurance for your family. Take into consideration what your family will need to pay taxes on your estate, your children's upbringing and education, and your family's needs after you're gone.

Fill out the Estate Letter of Instructions completely. Give your family as much information as you can possibly provide to ease their burden after you've gone. Speak with your family about your plans. Before you meet with them, draw up a list of all the subjects you wish to discuss. Tell them who each of your advisors is and inform them where your will, advance medical directives, and Estate Letter of Instructions are located. Explain the reasons for the choices you made and answer their questions.

Take two aspirin and call me in the morning!

My Rx

A will is a terrible place to keep secrets. Sit down with your family and discuss what is in your will. Tell them who the executor is and who gets what. Explain the reasons for your decisions to avoid fights and ill will after you're gone. Let's say that you have two children, Jack and Jim. Jack has a great job, but Jim is always struggling. So you leave Jim $150,000 and only $50,000 to Jack because Jim needs it more. If Jack doesn't learn about the difference until after you're gone, he may not fully understand your reasoning and it may create tension between them.

Estate planning is a complex area. Numerous state and federal laws can be involved. Hiring a good estate-planning attorney will be money well spent. An attorney can make sure that your will and all documents are written and executed properly. If you have young children, or one with special needs or who is extremely irresponsible or immature, you may want to establish trusts to limit, parcel out, or supervise how they receive their inheritances. Estate planning attorneys can establish these safeguards for you.

CHAPTER 19

NOT DOWNSIZING
IN RETIREMENT

THE AILMENT

For many people, retirement is the promised land. It's a time they've always dreamed of, when they no longer have to work and will finally have time to do as they please. To reach their goal, they played by the book: they saved, invested, and built up nice retirement funds. Now, after years of putting their families first, they get to focus on themselves and do what they want. Or so they think.

Retirees often struggle because retirement can be a dramatic change. It's not just trading a career for a life of leisure and large paychecks for smaller dividends. Excitement, responsibilities, challenges, growth, and prestige can all diminish. All of a sudden, you're not so busy and not constantly making important decisions. You're no longer in the center of all the action, but on the sidelines, out of the game.

To ease the transition, many people try to keep other aspects of their lives at the same level they enjoyed when they were working and their incomes were at their peaks. To fill the gaps, they try to remain active, eat well, take courses, entertain guests, and travel. It's not easy giving up what you have built, loved, and identified with. Many feel that all they have left is their pride, so they refuse to downsize. Though it's important to have a full life during your retirement and enjoy the fruits of your labor, it's just as important to make the necessary changes so that you can live reasonably comfortably for many years off of your retirement funds.

DIAGNOSIS

When you retire, your life will be different; you won't have the same needs. It becomes essential to make adjustments so you can get the most of your life. Because your income will be reduced, downsize the parts of your life that you no longer need. Downsizing will save you money, time, and aggravation.

The most important item to downsize is your home, because housing expenses are usually the largest item in your budget. When you retire, your choice of housing will determine your lifestyle. The lower your housing costs, the more money you will have available for other things.

VITAL SIGNS

Most retirees don't need to live in big houses with lots of rooms. The bigger the home, the more it costs to maintain. Plus, it takes much more work, which many retirees can no longer do. In addition to steeper mortgage payments or rents, bigger homes usually have higher property taxes, insurance premiums, maintenance, and utility costs. The money for those additional costs could be used to improve your lifestyle during your retirement years.

Although downsizing their homes will improve their financial health, many retirees can't make the move. They're comfortable in their homes, to which they may have strong emotional ties and attached wonderful memories. For years, their home was the center of their lives, the nest where they raised their family and the scene of many memorable events. They know all their neighbors and consider them friends.

Many retirees spent years improving their homes and making them exactly they way wanted. They landscaped, planted trees, and added extra rooms. Frequently, they did a lot of the work themselves. Now that their homes are finally completed, they don't want to leave. Many feel deeply rooted and too old to move. So they stay put. Unfortunately, many retirees are trapped in their expensive homes. After they pay their living expenses, they have no money left to enjoy anything else in their lives.

If retirees downsize by selling their homes and buying or renting smaller, less expensive ones, it can free substantial amounts of money that they can invest to generate income. Because many have lived in their homes for years, they have built up a lot of equity that can be earning money for them.

When my father retired, my parents had the choice to continue living in the family home or moving to a smaller residence. Had they stayed in their house, virtually all of their income would have been spent paying for and maintaining their home. It would have cut down on what they could do and they would never have been able to travel or expand their lives.

After we sat down and discussed their situation, my parents sold their house and used the proceeds to buy a smaller home in a retirement community. By downsizing, they eliminated their mortgage and home equity loan payments. Although they pay a small maintenance fee, their taxes, insurance, and utilities are considerably less. The money they saved can now be used to improve the quality of their lives in their retirement years.

When my parents moved, they became less isolated. At their retirement community, they take part in numerous cost-free activities and have made many new friends. Many of the new friends have backgrounds, careers, and interests that are similar to those of my parents.

Because their new friends are also retired, they understand each other's financial situation. They socialize, but not lavishly. They also participate in many activities together, which keeps their costs down. Living in their new community also enables them to live a comfortable lifestyle and to be more financially secure.

TREATMENT

By the time you retire, you don't want to have debt payments. If you do, you want them to be as small as possible. The ideal is to eliminate all of your debt.

Retirees should also downsize their cars. If they had two cars, they should think about selling one, which will bring in some cash and cut down their insurance and car maintenance costs.

Retirees should seriously consider obtaining reverse mortgages, which allow them to convert the equity in their homes into cash that they can use during their lives. A reverse mortgage is a loan that lets older homeowners covert a portion of the equity in their homes into a chunk of cash, monthly income, or a line of credit. The following are some of the important features of reverse mortgages:

- ☑ Borrowers usually must be at least 62 years old and own and occupy a single-family, one-unit dwelling as their principle residence.

- ☑ Some lenders will give reverse mortgages on two- to four-unit owner-occupied dwellings, some condominiums, cooperatives, planned unit developments, and manufactured homes.

- ☑ Reverse mortgage loans in amounts up to $625,000 may currently be granted. Check the limits beforehand because they are subject to change.

- ☑ Borrowers can receive reverse mortgage payments in a lump-sum payment, a line of credit, in installments, or various combinations thereof.

☑ Borrowers do not have to repay their reverse mortgage loan until their home is no longer the surviving borrower's principle residence.

☑ When the last borrower dies, sells the home, or moves from the home permanently, the reverse mortgage must be fully repaid, including all interest and other charges.

☑ The amount borrowers owe grows through time, because interest accrues and the borrowers are not making payments.

☑ If, after a reverse mortgage loan is repaid, equity remains in the home, that equity belongs to the borrower or his or her heirs.

☑ During the reverse mortgage term, the borrower continues to own the home.

☑ Borrowers are responsible for property taxes, insurance, and maintenance of their home. Their failure to keep up could make the balance of the loan due and payable.

☑ The IRS does not treat the loan advance as taxable income.

Reverse mortgages can be an alternative to downsizing or a compliment to downsizing. As an alternative, it can allow retirees to remain in their homes and receive a lump-sum payment, monthly payments, a credit line, or combinations of them all. Or reverse mortgages can be a compliment to downsizing, because when retirees sell their family homes, they can buy smaller homes and then get reverse mortgages on them.

My Rx

The most important change to make during your retirement is your housing. Although you should find ways to cut back on many of your expenses, housing is the most significant, because it takes up a giant portion of living expenses.

Reverse mortgages make great sense for many retirees. It allows them to convert the equity in their homes to money that can help them lead comfortable lives. If you're debating whether to get a reverse mortgage, ask yourself the following questions: Why would I want to pay an existing mortgage, when I can have a lender pay me? When will I get another chance to borrow money and not have to worry about paying it back? So, I recommend downsizing your home and then taking a reverse mortgage on your new place.

CHAPTER 20
NOT KNOWING WHAT WEALTH REALLY IS

THE AILMENT

When people build wealth, they can change. As they acquire more money, their vision can narrow, and they can lose sight of everything else, especially the bigger picture. As they devote their time to building fortunes, they begin to lose other aspects of their lives. They become obsessive and spend less time at home with their families. When they're home, they're disconnected—their minds are somewhere else. Financially, they prosper, but their families suffer. Their children often have problems, become resentful, and act out.

Although they work tirelessly and earn lots of money, many never truly enjoy the fruits of their success. Sooner or later, something crashes and they can't understand why it happened to them.

DIAGNOSIS

It's easy to get diverted. You can be moving smoothly on course, when something suddenly intervenes and before you know it you're headed in a new and different direction, not where you intended to go. Money frequently has that effect. When it enters the picture, it can throw everything off track.

Passion can also be a problem. When you want something deeply, you may go after it with all your heart. You focus on your objective, let nothing stand in your way, and devote yourself to reaching your goals. Passion is a great motivator, and the most successful people tend to be zealous. Their passion is contagious and attracts followers and supporters.

However, passion can also be blinding. When you are immersed in your passions, you may not be able to see clearly. You miss what is obvious to others, even when it is right before your eyes.

Making money can stir our passion. Once you start making it, it can be addictive. You can get lost in the process and intoxicated by success. Your new status, lifestyle, and all you can do, buy, and be can be mesmerizing. You can lose track of your original objectives—why you wanted to build wealth. Your need to make money can take over and everything else can get pushed aside.

VITAL SIGNS

Why do we try to build financial health? We all have different reasons, but for me it's to enjoy life, to be happy and fulfilled, and do the things I like. By making myself financially fit, I've been able to take good care of my family, eat well, travel, and help others. I've also been able to build a retirement fund that will enable my wife and I to live comfortably in retirement.

I work hard, but I also make it a point to enjoy my life. I don't want to be the richest corpse in the cemetery. At the end of my life, I don't want to regret that I didn't spend more time with my family, didn't help others, or didn't do what was most important to me.

I've worked with too many wealthy clients who lived frugally all the time. Most of them were miserable. Although they had no reason to worry about money, they constantly did. Worrying about money can really bring you down and ruin your physical health. It can color everything in your life. These clients were obsessed with building their wealth. They hoarded it and rarely spent it; they seldom enjoyed it. As soon as they died, their children swooped in, gobbled up their money, and spent it wastefully.

TREATMENT

As you build your financial health, enjoy it. Reward yourself for working hard, sacrificing, and living responsibly. Don't be extravagant and throw your money away, but find a happy balance between building wealth and enjoying some of what your success can buy.

Don't put off enjoying life until you retire. You may never reach that point. Spend time with your family while they're still living at home. Your time and experiences together will forge strong bonds and memories that they will pass on to their kids.

Invest your time in what is most important to you. Time is frequently more important than money, especially when you can spend it with your family and friends and doing what you love.

When you retire, do what you couldn't do when you were younger, things that you might not have been able to afford or had the time to do. Because you've worked so hard to build for your future, remember that your future has finally arrived. Take care of yourself and live a good life.

Set examples that you would like your children to follow; show them how it's done. Give your children and grandchildren the legacy of financial health. Children tend to follow their parents' example: when parents are financially responsible, their children usually are also. If parents are financially irresponsible, their children usually follow suit. Also show your children how to enjoy balanced lives. Let them see your example of how to build wealth and enjoy their lives while they're building it.

Show your children the nobility of work. Working is gratifying and builds the confidence, pride, and drive that breeds success. Put your children in situations in which they can succeed and enjoy the experience and rewards of their labor. Start with small tasks and move toward those that are larger and involve more responsibility. Clearly show them what to do and be sure to compliment and thank them when they do it well.

Understand the danger of easy money. When young people come into money that they didn't work hard to earn, it can have a destructive effect. Many lottery winners, athletes, or young inheritors go right through the funds they receive. Within five to 10 years, many are broke, because they never learned money management skills. However, when they earn money by working hard, sacrificing, and being financially responsible, it means more to them, so they protect and spend it more responsibly.

My Rx

Money is nothing but potential until it's converted to items such as food, shelter, travel, and charity. A $100 bill is just a small piece of paper until we use it to buy what we want or need. Plan ahead. Decide what you want most, what's of the greatest importance to you, and when you can afford it, think about buying or doing it.

I constantly tell my radio audience and my clients that you can't take your money with you when you die and that you should enjoy the money you worked hard to accumulate over the course of your life. Make smart choices to build and preserve your wealth, but remember that the wealth is to be enjoyed and used to benefit your life and that of your family, now and in the future.

Follow-Up Care

Thanks for reading this book and trying to improve your financial health. I know that I've given you much to think about and absorb. Don't try to apply it all at once. Instead, try a few of my suggestions, stick with them, and when you see how well they're working, try a few more.

Focus on your financial health. As you do, be patient and persistent. As I've emphasized, improving your financial fitness will require you to change some of your attitudes, habits, and approaches. In most cases, we're not talking about major overhauls, but only adjustments. At first, some changes—like so many new things we tackle—may be difficult, but keep trying. Don't give up. Before long, you will become more fiscally fit and will have truly improved your life.

INDEX

About the Author

Louis G. Scatigna, CFP, is a financial expert who excels at clearly explaining complex fiscal matters. Since 1983 he has been a financial advisor and a licensed investment broker. In 1987, Lou founded AFM Investments, Inc., a full-service financial planning, tax preparation, and investment firm in Howell, New Jersey, where he serves as the president and CEO.

For more than 10 years, Lou has hosted the top-rated radio program, *The Financial Physician*, in which he answers listeners' telephone questions about finances. Lou gives his audience straightforward advice and stresses the importance of financial responsibility and financial literacy. His unorthodox approach has made him a maverick who does not hesitate to question and challenge both trendy and traditionally accepted financial industry views. He warned of the present financial crises more than two years ago. Lou's radio programs can be found on his Website, *www.thefinancialphysician.com*. He also provides additional comments and advice on his daily blog (*http://thefinancialphysician .blogspot.com*).

At AFM Investments (800-732-5250), Lou provides financial advice to many families and specializes in senior financial issues. Lou's advice is built on rock-solid research and information and based on well-reasoned approaches that have consistently passed the test of time. He excels at explaining and demystifying complex financial matters and putting them in clear, direct language that everyone can quickly grasp.

A dynamic and popular speaker, Lou has been quoted in numerous newspapers, including *USA Today*. He has also been a frequent guest on New York City radio and TV programs. He has become a self-made multi-millionaire and philanthropist who is devoted to helping the less fortunate. Recently, he completed the pilot for a reality-television program called *Operation Rescue* that he hosts. Each week, audiences will see Lou putting together resources and rescuing actual families that are struggling through deep financial crisis and dire need. This feel-good, docudrama spotlights Lou's caring, resourcefulness, determination, and appeal.

A native of Howell, New Jersey, Lou is a graduate of Rutgers University. He is married to Susan, his high-school sweetheart, and they have two children, Matthew and Michelle. They currently reside at the Jersey Shore.

AFM Investments, Inc. is a full-service financial planning firm. All securities transactions are through Leigh Baldwin & Company, Member FINRA and SIPC. Registered Investment Advisory services are through Summit Alliance Financial.